ONE TO ONE

A Teachers' Handbook

PETER WILBERG

Australia Canada Mexico Singapore Spain United Kingdom United States

One to One
A Teachers' Handbook
Peter Wilberg

Publisher/Global ELT: *Christopher Wenger*
Executive Marketing Manager, Global ELT/ESL: *Amy Mabley*

Printed in the UK.
     6 7 8 9 10   06 05 04 03 02

For more information contact Heinle, 25 Thomson Place, Boston, MA 02210 USA,
or you can visit our Internet site at http://www.heinle.com

ISBN: 0 906717 61 2a

Acknowledgements
To Ille Becker, without whom this book would never have been written.
To Cynthia, for being a beacon light.
To my students, for some hard, but effective, lessons.
To the teachers at the Pilgrims Executive Centre, for their support.
To Mike Gordon who provided the illustrations and cartoons.

407
W664

Introduction

... Approach one-to-one on a one-to-one basis with each new student

One-to-one teaching offers the teacher both a considerable challenge and an unrivalled opportunity to accumulate observations on individual learning processes, needs and difficulties.

Working creatively from these observations the teacher will be engaged, like the student in a constant process of acquiring and learning new skills from experience and practice. In sharing some of my own observations and ideas therefore, my principal aim is to encourage others to do so themselves, and thereby bring about an end to the remarkable shortage of written material to guide and inspire teachers; both those who are new to, and those who are old hands in this field.

I hope that this book will also be helpful and stimulating to those whose job it is to organise, supervise or market one-to-one courses; encouraging the necessary investment of thought, care and facilities to bring ever-better returns to both school and student and professional satisfaction to the teacher.

The central question is the relationship between the skills that are practised and the language that is presented. Too often the skills work focuses on content and the language practice on form. One-to-one demands precisely the opposite: a language practice whose content is determined by the student, and skills training focused on language forms which can then serve the re-formulation of this content at a new level of performance.

What's so special about one-to-one?

One-to-one:

- is the number one choice for a large number of students

- is a large and important sector of the language training market

- is perhaps the oldest way in which people have chosen to learn a foreign language

- interaction is the basic paradigm of communication, the dyad

- is the least discussed subject in language teaching theory, though its principles are relevant to all teaching contexts

- is a most challenging test for the theory and practice of teaching, particularly in the areas of

    student-centred learning
    autonomous learning
    learner training
    teacher development
    discourse analysis
    specialised teaching

- teachers face an almost total lack of published materials written with them in mind. It is not very helpful to use course books with instructions such as *Get the students to stand in a circle.*

- needs the attention and experience of teacher trainers as well as teachers, if the latter are not simply to apply what they have learnt about class teaching to the job of one-to-one. That would be both difficult and dangerous.

Contents

1. Basic Principles

One-to-One teaching is different.

Class teaching is essentially artificial; we do not spend much of our lives addressing and controlling groups! One-to-one is essentially natural, the basic unit of our daily communication. Its essence is lack of artifice.

Basic Principles

One-to-one teaching is different. Different, that is, from conventional class teaching. This fact cannot be over-emphasised.

The basic principle of group teaching is that teacher input provides the language for student output. In an attempt to make group teaching more 'student-centred' this principle may be forgotten. Students may engage in all sorts of "communicative activities" without pre-teaching of new language. Communication becomes an end-in-itself and students complain about not being taught.

In teaching groups of businessmen this is a great danger. Textbooks and teachers both seem to aim at teaching students business rather than teaching them English, though it can safely be assumed that they know more about their own business than anyone can teach them.

This only highlights the problem faced in all group teaching, namely that it has to be based on some standard image of the learner and of learners' needs. In the case of business English teaching there is a standard image of 'the businessman'. In actual fact, however, there is very little in common between the language needs of say, a marketing man in the tobacco industry about to go to South America for important negotiations and an accounts manager needing English to obtain technical advice in using a new piece of software. While both of them may need to use English on the phone, their real needs will hardly be touched by simply giving them what passes as 'telephone English' on most business courses, namely making polite noises and obtaining the person you want to speak to. What counts is *who* exactly that person is; *what* the student will be talking about and needing to understand in the conversation. Effective English for telephone talk is not a few stereotyped phrases. It depends on the particular *content* that marks an individual student's particular job or situation.

What are we teaching?

To say that it is 'English' or 'Japanese' or 'French' is no answer at all in one-to-one, certainly not in teaching designed to meet the specific language needs of individuals.

To say that it is 'Business English' is a step forward. For 'language' is used not just to refer to national, regional and ethnic languages but also professional languages. But the question is 'which business?' Are we talking the language of management, marketing, sales, computers, production technology or what?

The World of Work, the World of English, and the World of the Individual are each vast domains. So also are the multiple languages of work, the languages of English and the languages of the individual: it is only where these domains overlap that the 'target' language is to be found.

The paradox is that businessmen do not need to be taught business language, their own language, any more than they need to be taught their mother tongue. Nor is it 'General English' they need. So we talk about 'communication skills' instead. But again, one assumes that a successful executive has proved those skills. Ah yes, but not in English. But what are English communication skills? Are we speaking of literacy in business communication? Of conventions of Business English as opposed to Business German or Business American? And again, which business? Which language? Which skills?

Is there anyone who can give a real answer to these questions, without paradox, except the *student*. Yet he or she, is the one we are supposed to be *teaching*.

This is another paradox. We can't teach unless we know what the student wants to communicate. But communication cannot develop without teaching.

The paradox is especially relevant to one-to-one teaching based on thorough-going 'needs analysis'. But 'needs analysis' can be a catchword by which we *avoid* instead of respond to the challenge of the paradox, in both theory and practice.

It must be emphasised that by "the language the student needs", a great deal more is meant than certain specialised vocabulary. Of course many one-to-one students do require specific and specialised vocabulary to do their jobs. It is important to recognise also, however, that they require certain grammatical forms, and, like all other students, an ability to use their voices, an awareness of pronunciation and stress features, and all the other things which we associate with a "general course".

The teacher's job is not to provide the communicative content but find out what it is and then select the language forms that match it. One-to-one allows the teacher to operate in this way. The student provides the content, the input. The teacher provides the form, the *language* that meets the student's communicative needs. Instead of *ending* with communication practice, one-to-one *begins* with it.

The first thing to do, then, is to get the student to *do* whatever he or she will *have* to do in real life. This then provides the teacher with the raw material to decide what the student needs to *learn*. Creating a communicative framework for student input I call 'formatting'. Analysing the linguistic forms present in (or missing from) this raw material I call 'auditing'. The procedure is therefore:

1. Find out the students' communicative needs

2. Create space for student input through real communication practice ('Formatting')

3. Analyse the student's linguistic needs ('Auditing')

An appropriate format for business students could be writing a report, role-playing a call, giving a presentation, dictating a letter. The starting point is the student telling us what he or she needs to do in real life.

Alternatively, or in addition, the student's input may take the form of company brochures, sample correspondence, etc. The language of this material also needs to be examined critically, if possible before the start of the course, and used as a guide to the language needs of the student. If he or she needs to write reports, no better basis for a course can be had than an actual report from his or her company, or one that the student writes for the teacher, or *both.* If the student provides written material but requires oral skills the former may still provide the basic content and some of the forms appropriate to the latter.

The critical examination of this material then provides the basis for teaching. But the aim of teaching is not to teach the student his or her business but to raise awareness of language forms and their role serving communicative content.

To do this, these forms must be made visible. One way of doing this is to **reformulate** the student's input. Instead of a haphazard, interruptive correction *of* the student's language we reformulate it in a structured way *for* the student. This can be done orally, sentence by sentence, with the student recording our reformulation of each utterance. Or it can be done in writing, on the board or in our own time after the lesson. Either way the result is a model of language tailored to the student's communicative and linguistic needs.

The next step is to make the student aware of the language forms, and able to audit the language models for him- or herself. This means the ability to identify the new language it contains and practise it. The model could be company material provided by the student, who will most likely be familiar with the content but unaware of the forms, the language used to express this content.

Rather than extracting this language for the student and presenting it to him or her as if from nowhere, our job is to train the students to identify and extract this language *for themselves,* to pass on the very same awareness and skills that we as teachers apply in analysing the language in a text or transcript.

We move from the whole (whole text, whole transcript) to the parts. Having become aware of the importance of a particular language form (e.g. the role of a certain tense, function, or structure) in the model or reformulated text, the teacher can then provide further input designed to reinforce and practise this language, using coursebooks or specially pre-pared material. The purpose of this input, it must be remembered, is to aid the student in the next stage of re-formulating his or her *own* output. For example the student now re-constructs or re-drafts a report *using* the language revealed in the audit stage, and based on the teacher's re-formulation or other model material.

We test the student therefore, on what he or she has been taught. The test is automatically both communicative and linguistic. This is important because there is a lot of talk about 'progress' made by students on one-to-one courses and how to measure it, if it exists at all.

'Progress' and 'improvement' are sheer abstractions. One-to-one means teaching the student to *do* specific things. We cannot measure a student's 'general' improvement, but only his or her ability to do the things we have taught.

Most one-to-one teaching is done with adult students who have immediate use for the language which they are studying. It is usually those people who are already operating as managers who are studying to improve their "management English". This has an important conse-quence for the teacher. All teachers, but perhaps language teachers more than most, feel the need to correct mistakes. Accuracy is frequently given a very high priority. Many students expect every mistake to be corrected, and, because of their previous learning experience, also give accuracy high priority. But if the student is to be functional in English during, or immediately after, a course, accuracy becomes less important. The main criterion moves to the student's ability to express his or her meaning effectively. It helps if both teacher and student are explicitly aware of the fact that criteria which are different from, but as demanding as, formal accuracy, are being employed. For students who have an immediate use for the language they are studying, the communication may be *defective,* providing it is *effective.* It is this criterion which the teacher should employ.

We cannot wait for, or even assess the statistical probability of a student needing to use language taught on a course in general conversation (whatever that is!). In a lot of cases it will be nil. A useful analogy here is playing the piano. If someone teaches me to play a particular piece, the test of my 'progress' is playing that piece. Learning to play it may indeed improve my general ability, but there is no way of testing or measuring *that* because *all* tests are specific, including most 'general' English tests, for what they usually measure is the student's ability to fill in words on a bit of paper in a context that has nothing to do with his or her real life outside the classroom.

The product and the test of one-to-one teaching is a *piece of work* done by the student and requiring that he or she reformulate his or her own content at a new level of awareness, skill and linguistic competence.

The test need not be to re-enact the *same* role play, or to re-write the same report or letter. Nor need the result be perfect but can, instead, provide a basis for further stages of reformulation and auditing. In fact the test may be a test of auditing skills as such; a listening test for example, in which the focus is on form rather than content, on learning to 'pick up' language as well as understand communication, or to do both at the same time.

Reformulation, whether by student or by teacher, may also involve **re-formatting.** This can mean simply typing something out, transferring something from tape to text, or from text to table or graph. It can literally mean using the appropriate format, for example for a letter or report. The teacher may re-format a piece of student writing or a transcript to highlight the language points which arise in reformulating it: offering choices of language, substitution patterns or simply adding language notes. The student can be asked to transcribe a taped dialogue, or transfer a presentation onto cards.

Coursebooks themselves are nothing but a combination of formatted material, and auditing exercises involving information transfer or re-formatting. Even a simple transformation drill is an exercise in reformulation, and a cut up 'jigsaw', an exercise in reformatting. Transferring language extracted from a text or transcript to a notebook or file is also an example of reformatting. Students are notoriously bad in making organised notes. They are careless of formats as well as language forms. That is why coursebooks are so tempting—they offer both, without any work. But it is precisely the sort of work that goes into a coursebook, particularly one for specialised English, that the student can benefit most from doing: producing his or her own *personalised* data file or coursebook, including model texts tailored in terms of topic, content and form to the **individual.**

Much conventional teacher training is devoted to helping the teacher with what we might call class management—the organisation of time, setting up of group work, and the development and control of relationships within the group. None of these skills is relevant to one-to-one teaching. There is, however, a comparable, and equally important set of skills. There is a temptation to think no "group dynamics" is involved in one-to-one teaching, and that there is only a single relationship involved in the classroom activities. This is not true. The teacher assumes different roles in class teaching—instructor, controller, timekeeper, language authority, and, in school teaching, discipline authority. In a quite different, but similar, way the teacher assumes many different roles in the one-to-one classrooom—colleague, 'mirror', friend, authority on language form (though no longer on content).

One essential difference, however, from classroom teaching is that it is no longer the teacher who initiates all the role changes. The one-to-one teacher's task is much more to respond to changes of mood and demands imposed by the student, rather than to act as manager and controller of the classroom.

Just as the classroom teacher needs to be aware of why each activity is being conducted in the way it is, so the one-to-one teacher needs to be explicitly aware of the personal role (s)he is fulfilling in relation to the student at any time.

In some ways it is more convenient for the teacher to teach classes than individuals. It is unrealistic to expect individual, personal attention while you are in a class of 30. Everyone in such a situation accepts that some of his or her individual needs or characteristics need to be subordinated to those of the group. This means the teacher can, however irresponsible it may be, ignore certain difficulties on the basis that they are too peculiar to one individual. No such escape exists in one-to-one teaching. Teachers who are used to teaching groups and are approaching one-to-one teaching for the first time may find it helpful to pause for a few moments with a blank piece of paper. Write down as many differences as you can between individuals—the ways in which one person is different from another.

This list is, of course, almost endless. And many of the differences you have written down will affect an individual's abilities and attitudes to learning. Even teachers who are regularly involved in one-to-one teaching can usefully make a list of this kind from time to time to remind them exactly how different people are, and how many personal differences need to be taken into account in the one-to-one teaching situation.

Most one-to-one students will bring to the course a set of expectations which may vary from realistic and helpful to confused and destructive. In many, perhaps most cases, their earlier language learning experience is unlikely to have prepared them well for the approach most appropriate to their present needs. For many one-to-one students their needs are much more specific than when they studied languages at school, or in any form of general course. One of the teacher's functions is to help students to identify their language needs. For most one-to-one students, for example, it would be true that a set of job-specific language functions would be of considerable use to them; most will be helped by an awareness of the language used in relatively formal meetings, and most will need to acquire the language to help them "soften" the direct expression of their views. If their previous learning has concentrated on vocabulary and grammar, or on such traditional language skills as reading and writing, the teacher will need to help the student to see and express these alternative language needs.

Many students may need to read articles or reports in English. The skill required, however, will bear little relation to the skill of reading a text in a language teaching book. Language teaching texts are frequently followed by comprehension questions and exercises; a student is more likely to need the ability to make notes on the basis of an article so that he can, for example, give an oral report of it to colleagues.

In a similar way, many students may need to prepare talks or reports in English but the skills required for this kind of preparation are very different from those required to produce a school essay.

Preparing notes from a report or article involves selecting and sequencing the key lexical items (meaning-carrying words and phrases); the initial preparation for the production of a talk or report involves starting from certain words and phrases. In both cases the lexis is of considerably more importance than what language teachers traditionally think of as "grammar".

It is worth noting that this idea—the centrality of lexis—also suggests a way of teaching which is particularly appropriate for people with a business background. "Brainstorming" is now a common management technique, and involves listing the key ideas in a problem or argument, before sequencing them for a particular purpose. This idea conforms to one of the basic ideas of this book—namely that the student is the expert on the content, and the teacher the expert on language form.

Differences

One-to-one is a unique teaching situation with unique potential. It offers a unique challenge to both teacher and student. Since it is often thought of as a restrictive situation, let's begin by listing the things you *can* do in one-to-one that you *can't* do in groups.

Basic principles

These highlight the differences between one-to-one and group teaching and form the basis for the various practical and creative possibilities that this handbook will describe.

Taking only two of these points is enough to reveal the fundamental difference in one-to-one.

'Go at the student's own pace.' This is both possible and necessary in one-to-one. Possibly because there is no class to be managed. Necessary because every individual has a different pace, and only by responding to this pace will he or she feel space for learning. Communicative space means a balance and rhythm of speech and silence, address and response. Some people respond slowly and thoughtfully, others react quickly, and possibly with less thought. Slowness should not be mistaken for dullness; speed does not always imply carelessness. Individuals are different.

It helps to think of one-to-one as a dance. Your student is your partner. 'Go at the student's own pace' sounds simple. As simple as learning to waltz. Are you concentating on your own steps that are too big? As in the dance, it is no exaggeration to say that every move counts. Every position counts. Physical positions and movements carry messages in communication. With your body language you may not be going at your student's pace even though you think you are. This leads to the second point. 'Be in authentic communication with the student at all times'. This sounds obvious also and yet it is fundamental. Remember that in one-to-one the student has a double task. You teach *by* communicating with your student. But you also communicate personally with your student *through* your teaching. Therefore the student has both to take in what you teach, *and* to respond to your communication *as* communication, in other words to respond to the signals and messages it contains. If you regard yourself as 'only' teaching, and forget that you are also transmitting a whole variety of messages through your words, tone of voice and body language you will be cut off from yourself and your student. If you respond to your student only as a teacher and pay no heed to the signals and messages you are getting you cannot help him or her to use language more effectively in communication. One-to-one is an essentially personal activity.

Many students want English for social and professional situations. One-to-one *is* both a social and a professional situation. Everything either of you does is a communicative act. Communication is going on even if you are both silent or doing a repetitive drill. Getting on with your student is not a matter of like or dislike but of sensitive adjustment and awareness of pace, rhythm and step. As dance partner your job is to guide, but not to rush, grip too firmly, confuse or tread on your student's mental toes.

Teaching and Learning

Class teaching tends ultimately to be based on a theory of what different learners have in common. Beliefs about what is best for learners continue to reproduce and multiply, as do approaches to teaching. One-to-one on the other hand, demands not theories but powers of observation and a basic attitude of openness that is 'beyond belief'. The focus in one-to-one is the *individual,* and the role of theory is to offer us a language with which to understand the individual and meet his or her learning needs, in all their diversity.

In this sense a book on one-to-one is a contradiction in terms. No book can provide a recipe or course outline for a particular student. What it can do is to highlight the differences between one-to-one and class teaching, to describe the unique challenges of one-to-one teaching, and provide strategies and tools for what might be called 'the individual approach' to teaching.

There are no 'tried and tested' methods that guarantee success with every student, or with every teacher. Nor can we be sensitive to our student's uniqueness if we have no respect for our own personality, preferences and inclinations. 'Marriages' between teachers and students are not made in heaven, nor can they be 'purified' of feelings of antipathy, boredom, irritation or even anger. Why indeed should they be if what we are to teach is the language of one-to-one interaction: the paradigm of communication itself in both everyday life and professional business?

We cannot stop ourselves making judgements of our students whether negative or positive. We should be aware of these judgements as of our own feelings towards him or her. For they can either help or distort and hinder the learning process. Burying them under a veneer of cool professionalism doesn't help. Far better to ask the question: *What can I learn from my student, both as a professional and as a person?*

Once again, a good teacher is a good student: of his or her own feelings and observations as much as anything else. Our responsibility is not to guarantee our students success but to be responsive, and like our student, to learn from experience. The teacher teaches and facilitates, yet does not create or substitute for the *learner's* learning. The teacher remains responsible for applying his or her *own* learning in the teaching situation.

One-to-one teaching gives the satisfaction of any shared learning process that takes place between two people under the banner of self-responsibility and professional development. It can be hard work, and painful, but it can be fun. It is always rich in potential and meaning, and naturally so. It should not need to be 'personalised' but only stripped of the artificiality of so much TEFL theory. It also contains an irreducible element of ambiguity and a dimension of unknowables that cannot be purged by a crystalline architecture of technique, style or methodology.

The inspirations that filter down 'vertically' from the region of applied linguistics are a poor substitute for a 'horizontal' sharing of observations, experience and ideas between teachers, who, doing one-to-one are quite literally on the front line of empirical research into what helps individuals to listen, speak, and learn.

If there are 'Masters' of the Art of one-to-one they are probably amongst the least academic in approach, and the most gifted with qualities of inner calm, enthusiasm, and sense of self that does not allow itself to be intimidated, masked or constricted by the necessity to see themselves in the role of 'teacher'. The secret is to use the role as a vehicle of authentic personal communication rather than as a defence against it. Only in this way does one-to-one cease to be the prison that teachers sometimes feel it to be.

Things you can do in one-to-one that you can't do in groups

- Go at the student's own pace

- Be in authentic communication with the student at all times

- Use input, materials and biographical data supplied by the student for language work in a more intensive way

- Monitor the student's communication, progress and errors on a continuous basis

- Work with student presentations without worrying about time

- Give students opportunities to record themselves, handle and control equipment and aids such as telephones, cassette recorders, computers etc.

- Give students the task of transcribing recorded material from listening and in their own time

- Make extensive use of 'close-up' aids such as Cuisenaire rods, and cards

- Give each student his or her own 'in-tray' and choices in what to do and how to do it

- Gather and collate material to suit individual needs

- Make use of L1 in a variety of ways . . . even if you don't know the language

- Prepare tailor-made material for lessons

- Arrange visits and trips to suit the individual

- Prepare self-access work on an individual basis

- Handle lessons with greater spontaneity, naturalness and responsiveness to the individual personality, level, and 'style' of the student

- Prepare for specific real-life situations

- Make extensive use of dictation and student board-work (see pp. 125 and 102)

- Take breaks at any time

- Give each student a unique retrospective coursebook and/or tape to take away

- Plan the pattern of the working day with the student, and offer choices

2. A basic working paradigm

In one-to-one teaching the emphasis is on the student providing the content, and the teacher providing the form. This means a basic paradigm radically different from the traditional present— practise—produce of much classroom language teaching.

Initially students on one-to-one present their needs, through pre-course information and needs-analysis, possibly supported by interviews early in their course. Too often, however, the course itself is relatively conventional and involves teaching pre-selected material to the student. This is not the tailor-made, individualised response one-to-one demands.

The central axiom for one-to-one is that throughout the whole course space needs to be created for student input; there must be opportunities for continuous re-definition of needs. The basic strategy must not be intensive, pressurised 'teaching' but rather creating space for learning. The approach involves:

creating space for student input and learning

structuring this space ('formatting')

re-presenting student content in appropriate forms ('re-formulation')

analysing and making the student aware of language forms

('auditing')

All these activities must be carried out within a framework of authentic communication between student and teacher. It is the relationship between two individuals which forms the basis for all the teaching and learning activities.

A basic working paradigm

Why isn't he more responsive?

Why doesn't she make more of an attempt?

Why just sit there waiting for me to perform?

Why can't he show more charm?

Why doesn't she show a bit more enthusiasm?

Despite the idea of equality between teacher and student in a learner-centred approach, these typical reactions of teachers in one-to-one amount to one thing:

Why doesn't the student live up to my demands and expectations?

Responsibility to the student does not mean guaranteeing his or her progress. This would imply an impossible omnipotence on the teacher's part. Nor can it mean in any way trying to force a student to reach goals that we have set, or fulfil our needs or expectations.

Responsibility is response-ability

Our responsiveness as teachers is adapting to the *student's* personality, expectations, motivations and moods. This response-ability does not end with 'needs analysis' and the preparation of neatly ordered lists of functions and structures. *Defining* the student's linguistic and communicative needs is one thing. *Teaching* is another, and *caring* that the student really *learns* something durable from our teaching is something else again. This is where response-ability comes in.

How to respond to what appears to be lack of motivation in the student?

How to respond to the stereotyped expectations of the student?

How to adapt to the learning experience and habits of the student?

In other words:

How to learn what this particular student is trying to teach us?

It is all too easy to polarise with a student. I well remember a particular student who sat rigidly, with a totally immobile face during each lesson. All my attempts at elicitation and energisation failed. The more resistance I met, the more energy I put in until I found myself virtually doing a dance around the student. I reacted to his lack of energy with excess energy. I polarised with him.

This continued to the point of despair, at which point I finally surrendered. By this time we had already completed day 4 of a 5-day course. Desperate that he should feel some tangible result, I prepared a set of cards for him to take away as revision and review aids covering all the language we had worked on. But the next morning, instead of bouncing in with my usual energy I went his way. I sat myself down calmly and solidly in my chair, adopting his stance and mood. Instead of energetic activity we engaged in a long, slow sequence of drills. And, for the first time in the week, we began to get somewhere.

Reflecting on this experience taught me several lessons in dealing with the apparently immovable or unmotivated student:

- Do not polarise with the student but identify with his or her stance . . . tune in.

- Instead of putting out limitless energy in the lesson, downgrade your own output, go into a lower gear.

- Challenge the student, and earn his or her respect by work put into preparation. In this case the student was very impressed by the care put into the cards; much more impressed than by my dance, which was out of tune with his personality.

- With this student there was a huge gulf between the analysis of communicative needs, and his own learning style and expectations which in no way matched an oral/aural communicative approach but demanded instead an old-fashioned grammar-based course. He enjoyed, and clearly benefited from, the drills. This was what he believed in, and therefore this was what worked for him.

  Had he stayed another week we could have worked further, using and adapting a traditional teaching approach *to* his communicative needs. My conclusion here is thus that what counts is above all finding the teaching style that suits the student. Do not assume that communicative needs can only be met by a so-called communicative approach. The latter is fine in theory but pointless if it doesn't work. You cannot re-educate a student in learning theory on a short-intensive course.

- Adapting to the student's stance is very much a question of speech and posture. A student with a slow, reflective speech style should not be expected to adopt a new, fast and informal style in L2. Nor should a highly spontaneous and rapid speaker, however inaccurate, be dulled into slow, over-monitored robot English.

Stereotyped expectations

It cannot be too often repeated that coursebooks are aimed at an abstract 'average student'. This applies no less to Business English materials, which are based on a stereotyped image of 'the business executive'. This stereotyped businessman is almost invariably in sales or marketing, and has no other interests outside his job, to which he is fully committed.

The reality in one-to-one often proves different. The moment we leave the world of the registration form and come to face with the real individual, a different face begins to appear. The face of a person and human being, more or *less* committed to his or her job or company, more or *less* happy with his or her life, and more or *less* interested in entering the cardboard world of textbook stereotypes.

True motivation might vary from genuine fanatical commitment to a product or company on the one hand, to simply taking a break from routine or having a holiday on the other. In between there is a whole spectrum of motivation:

- The student who enjoys being the centre of attention, who finds relief and diversion from loneliness or boredom in one-to-one.
- The student who is sent by a boss: for example the overworked secretary expected to double as translator.
- The student who is anxious about his or her future career, who thinks that English is a necessary accomplishment.
- The student whose current communicative needs are not as important as future ones. For example a student who dreams secretly of abandoning a present job and going to live in an English-speaking country.
- The student whose motivation is intrinsic, and based on a genuine interest in the culture of the foreign language.
- The student whose interest in the language is academic and not really for everyday communication at all.
- The student whose competence exceeds his or her confidence. For example a highly advanced student whose only limitation is lack of confidence and who needs to be weaned away from dependence on a teacher (eg by teaching self-study or acquisition skills).
- The student who is attracted by the prestige or marketing allure of an expensive one-to-one course; who wants to be in with the best.
- The student who wishes to compete with a friend, colleague or subordinate whose foreign language skills are embarrassingly superior.
- The student whose real learning problems are principally psychological and hopes for a magic cure from one-to-one.
- The student whose real interests and involvement with life have very little to do with his or her job, or stated 'communicative needs'.

The more we turn away from textbooks and start using the biographical material of teacher and student, the more the real needs of the student become clear. This way we can teach the real person and not a stereotype.

Ethics and professionalism

An authentic and professional relationship between teacher and student is based on shared responsibility. 'We're in this together' should be the basic motto. Within this relationship, the role and degree of initiative of the teacher can vary considerably according to the level, maturity, confidence, intelligence and independence of the student.

The teacher may be required to act like a parent to a dependent 'infant' beginner, using games, realia and picture-books. At the other extreme the teacher may take the role of a cool professional consultant, offering learner training and helping the student to plan his or her language project with a long-term learning strategy.

In between these two extremes the teacher may be coach, controller, conductor, counsellor and fill many other roles.

Whatever the teacher's role, however, there is a sharing of roles, and of responsibility. This relationship is easily distorted however when teachers are *sold* to students by an employer as guarantors of learning. Much of the anxiety of one-to-one teachers, and the artificial guilt that lurks in their unconscious, arises from the fact that in buying a teacher from a school students are led to believe that they can *buy* learning. The money is paid. The teacher 'delivers' the learning. In fact, of course, what the teacher delivers is teaching. Learning a language is not like buying a product. It is buying a service, not a person.

The relationship of teacher and student is in fact a constant *negotiation* of responsibility. The more the student progresses, the more responsibility for learning he or she takes. Conversely, every step forward, almost every word uttered by the student, is an assumption of responsibility . . . or response-ability . . . in the foreign language.

There is no reason why the marketing of language courses should not encourage positive expectations. But, and this is a big 'but' it is important to recognise that schools are selling a *product*, while teachers are not. The teachers have a responsibility to respond to the individual student, to learn from their mistakes, to prepare materials, but there is no way they can *guarantee* successful learning. Schools which promise this are expecting the impossible of their teachers.

The professional ethics of teaching are at the same time the most obvious feature of the *discourse* of teacher and student, which is this constant negotiation and re-negotiation of responsibility, and not a relationship of buying and selling. Of course teachers have their own share in this responsibiltiy; that is to be as responsive as possible to what makes this student different from all others, both as a student and as a person, and not to see him or her as just another 'client'. This is where the teacher's ethics and professionalism merge.

Creating space for learning

Let's not forget the unusualness of the job. Where else but in schools of English are two individuals who have never met in their lives before and may have nothing in common expected to spend a major part of each working day together in a confined space, and do this for several weeks. Even secretaries or business partners are not obliged to do this, and even if they are, they are certainly not contracted to really be *with* each other the whole time, constantly engaged in some sort of purposeful work or communication.

The danger is that not only will the physical space appear more and more confining, but that on a more fundamental level the psychological and personal space of the individuals will be compressed, threatened, and contracted in response. This withdrawal/contraction syndrome can set in fairly soon after the course has begun, and despite good intentions and the most amiable interaction between teacher and student, block the energies of both and stunt the learning progress.

The most valuable advice I can give in the form of a summary tip is therefore this: CREATE SPACE FOR LEARNING. This means both physical and psychological space, intellectual and emotional space. In an ideal world of course the actual size of the classroom space allotted for one-to-one work would be greater. The typical 'cell' that most schools provide is . . . small.

Within a larger space one would want to see a division of areas corresponding to the variety of styles of work and practice modes that the course can and should combine. Thus for example: an area for self-access work including resource material and a *separate desk* for the student. An area for 'pseudo-passive learning' with an armchair and headphones, and an armchair also for the teacher (adjacent not opposite!) who may wish to give relaxation exercises, tell stories, or offer suggestopedic 'concert readings' at the end of the day (or beginning). Between the armchairs of course, a coffee table. This may sound a little coddling or excessive, but why? Is there an office in the world without an armchair/coffee table/space for relaxed conversation, or reading?

Some schools may have a coffee room, a reception area or even a video room with armchairs. Study the physical provisions of your school and don't be afraid to be 'creative'; either using more than one room where possible, or borrowing furniture . . . armchairs for example, and using them in your classroom. If you are working at home or thinking of starting a school all the better. You can plan your use of space right from the start, and design a conducive learning environment for student and teacher. The question of creating space is discussed again in the chapter on preparation (see pages 69 to 75).

It seems that in England above all, we tend to ignore the relevance, the meaning, of exteriors, of creating a positive *suggestive context* for business and educational interaction, of putting care and consideration into space. This is an aesthetic issue too. Bare walls or tatty posters, spartan furnishing and uncomfortable chairs should not be acceptable to students or teachers themselves. They will certainly not go unnoticed, consciously or subconsciously, by managing directors or anyone used to Continental standards of office design. Again, it may seem silly, but should not be necessary to point out, that a good office or pleasant living room contains plants.

I shall return again to the importance of such 'gross' material things as oxygen for the learning process, but having worked in schools where this was, and still is, considered as a luxury, let me put in a plea for a green revolution in EFL. Of course a revolution is not necessary. One plant, strategically located, not only provides oxygen but also a pleasant focus for the eye and for the mind, seeking rest from its preoccupation with textbooks and needing space to think, to reply, to engage in creative and productive *reverie*.

The capacity and opportunity for reverie is in my view a basic condition for learning. Reverie is in itself a sort of psychic space opened up within time, as it were: a psychological time-space allowing a constant subconscious integration and absorption of material that might otherwise go in one ear and out the other. It is a state of mind that students manage more easily to sustain in the group classroom, where, despite teachers' tricks or protests, the individual may give himself or herself permission to be 'passive' for long periods, though by no means necessarily at the expense of concentration or inner alertness.

The one-to-one situation on the other hand, would seem to intensify the pressure on the student to be 'active' in an over-focused way, allowing no room for the mental rests and expansion of consciousness that reverie involves. The teacher must therefore be especially conscious of pacing: the spacing in time (psychological as well as clock-time) of the work. Nowadays more and more teachers are discovering the value of music, physical exercise, and guided relaxation techniques as stress-reducers in the classroom. But essentially it is the teacher's own ability to feel that he or she **has** time, and can **give** time that creates space for learning.

This feeling may not be easy to nurture and sustain on one-to-one courses which are billed as 'intensive' and often advertised to promote exaggerated expectations, but the soundest way to achieve it is to let the student determine the pace, intervening to alter it only where energy seems to be getting low or concentration too intense and contracted.

In terms of activities it is vital to give writing, silent reading and pleasure listening their place in each day's lessons. It is much more difficult for a one-to-one teacher to appear to do nothing and just let the student get on with something, yet this is just what is required. More important than the quantity of **TTT** (teacher talking time) is the amount of **SSS** (student silent space). The teacher may indeed not be passive at all but reading, story-telling, dictating or presenting new language. That is not the point, but rather that the teacher, whatever (s)he is doing or not doing, can carry and inwardly support **SSS**.

You may be a teacher who enjoys dramatic activities or prefers a meditative studious approach. Whatever your preferences for types of activity, adjust them to your student's own way and pace. Above all: never be prompted by the 'demands of time' or the need to 'fill time' to rush or overload. On the contrary concentrate on doing everything just a little bit more slowly, more 'spaciously', more 'graciously'. *Give* time, for that is what the job is all about.

"JUST TIME FOR A QUICK DRILL, I THINK!"

Reverie, space, must be nourished of course. Teacher and student must be both able to draw nourishment, the sustenance of meaning from the task at hand.

A learning exchange

This brings us straight to the heart of the so-called 'communicative' approach to teaching as it applies particularly to one-to-one. For the one-to-one experience is one in which one is constantly reminded that *meaning* is not embedded either in words or texts on the one hand, or in goals and career objectives on the other. What brings language, and language learning activities to life in one-to-one is the inter-personal relationship of teacher and student. The meaning is not there, somehow 'given', and needing only to be elicited. It is quite the reverse. Language and language activities possess meaning in the classroom in so far as they serve to elicit it from the inter-personal dynamic, the meeting of two individuals in the here and now. This *can* be forgotten in group teaching, where fun, games and frequent partner changes may disguise the fact that it is the inner encounter of individuals *as individuals* (and not as 'students') that provides the flesh and blood of meaning.

In one-to-one we become far more aware of the 'inner curriculum'. The meeting of teacher and student is a meeting of two worlds, that of the teacher and that of the student. Whatever is done in the classroom is an echo and symbol of this meeting and should not be an attempt to escape from the here-and-now and to superimpose one world upon the other.

The fact that we are teachers and that the student or company may be paying a lot of money for our services should not blind us to the fact that we are learners too, and that one-to-one is in essence a sort of learning exchange.

This means two things. Firstly it means that we are capable of making the same sort of mistakes that our students' make: of misjudging the language we need, of over-reliance on authority, bad habits and handling of situations, pride and timidity and so on.

Secondly it means that we are reliant on input. As one teacher put it succinctly: *I know the language, but they know their jobs.* The question is, however, do we know their language and can we be expected to? Certainly we cannot be experts in all fields and all languages. But like our students we can learn, and learn enough to do our job well, from meaningful input.

In fact we have a distinct advantage. For since our job is to teach others language skills, in obtaining the input *we* need to go on, we are also doing our job by giving the student an opportunity to practise those skills. The same is also true for the student. In providing us with input, in *teaching* us the 'target language', the student learns to do his or her job *in* it.

One-to-one is, therefore, essentially not a one-way teaching process beginning with teacher presentations and ending with free practice on the part of the student, but a developing dialogue in which what the *student* presents and what *we* learn is just as important. For this is the true aim of the students: to present and re-present themselves, their companies, products and services, their skills and qualities, using the medium of L2.

Formatting

The starting point is to create space for student input: silence, a blank page, a blank card or blank tape.

If we as teachers rush in and fill these blanks we are in danger of blotting out space for *student* input. If we do nothing, no input may come. So we need some structure, some aids, and some equipment. We need language and an approach to teaching that provides structured spaces or 'formats' for student input. Our task is that of formatting, rather than presenting.

It is not the teacher's job to dictate the content of communication to the student. On the contrary it is the student who should dictate content according to the sorts of things he or she needs to *say* in real life. Formatting means creating space for the student to input the content of communication. A format is a framework of communication that offers this space, allowing the student to determine the content and context of a written or oral text, independently of textbooks and text-tapes.

An example of a format can be anything that serves the aim of creating space for **authentic student input** rather than mere 'language practice'.

A basic working paradigm

Auditing

What are we actually doing when we 'read' or 'listen'? These macro-skills actually break down into numerous micro-skills which are also the basis of speaking and writing. For the individual student in one-to-one we need to be sensitive to the weakness or absence of these micro-skills; to what the student is *not* doing when reading or listening.

These skills need to be trained. It is their weakness or absence that prevents students from naturally acquiring language, turning the so-called receptive skills into active ones. Micro-skills involve the student in *auditing*, as well as learning to understand language. This means focusing the ear and the eye on form as well as content, and learning through discovery rather than explanation.

It is often said that before students are able to hear a sound they must be taught to speak it. In fact there are many students who are perfectly capable of using, say, a third person **'-s'** but never get into the habit of so doing because it is not reinforced by natural acquisition through listening. Why? Because the students still do not *hear* it.

Reading meaning and listening to words is not enough. Students need training in reading structures and morphology, and in hearing sounds and syllables. Without this training the search images they project will literally blind them to the word on the page (eg the article that literally is not seen) and to the sound in the air (the contraction or liaison that is not expected and thus makes no sense to the ear). Auditing involves two types of skill:

- The identification *of* language and sonic forms.
- Identification *with* these forms in speech and writing.

So-called 'active' and 'passive' skills are misnamed. The 'passive' or receptive, skills are no less active than the active ones.

They are identification skills of the first type. Production skills are in turn based on identification skills: on listening to oneself, 'reading' one's own mind, and auditing one's own 'inner' or 'pre'-speech *activity*. The micro-skills of auditing are applied in speaking and writing. They must also be trained through listening and reading.

Auditing is listening for form, and reading for form, rather than content. Identification of features of language and speech. The micro-skills of identification are applied in the macro-skills of reading, writing, speaking and listening.

The objective is to replace the teaching *of* language by a teacher with the training of students in the *skills* possessed by the teacher. These teacher skills are 'auditing' skills: the ability to recognise, recall, and thus reproduce language forms. I see one-to-one teaching as language skills training in this sense rather than language teaching. Auditing skills allow natural acquisition to take place by encouraging awareness of *how* things are said rather than just *what* is said. In ESP work the content is familiar to the student; what he or she lacks is the 'how' and not the 'what' of what is to be said.

Micro-skills

What, then, is a 'micro-skill' exactly? Skills are applied knowledge. Application means making choices. Language skills are based also on applying knowledge in action ie on making choices. This applies as much to 'receptive' as to active skills, for in interpreting sounds and words we also choose from a range or field of possible meanings.

Though for the native speaker these choices are more or less unconscious, they are nevertheless guided by beliefs and expectations. Though we do not normally focus our attention on these, they are no less 'conscious' for that, for if we decide to do so, we can. To oppose natural acquisition and unconscious assimilation to learning based on conscious cognitive skills and concepts is a mistake.

It is equally mistaken to oppose 'communicative skills' and competence to linguistic *drills* and competence. Students want grammar, not because they fail to recognise the importance of communicative practice, but because they see that communicative skills are based on making the right choices and that grammar drills train them in the micro-skills necessary to do this. They understand more than some teachers that language is just as much related to thought, and to *finding* the word, as it is to communication, and *using* the word.

As teachers we know that language colours and shapes communication, that form shapes content. This does not mean that explanation of concepts should replace communicative practice, but simply that conscious awareness and application of language is the goal, and basis even of so-called 'unconscious learning' methods. Communication cannot be taught. Language teaching is skills training. And drills do teach valuable skills. We use or rely on reading, writing, speaking and listening skills to 'drill' the micro-skills and mental skills that contribute to reading, writing, speaking and listening. This is a paradox but not an obstacle, or a reason for dismissing drills or grammar. Repetition, recall, substitution, transformation, sequencing, question formation, choice of register, short responses etc are not just types of drill; they are also micro-skills.

Drilling is not 'drumming in'; it is getting the student to make choices. The communication between teacher and student is authentic because it is about those choices, and because it carries over in a quite natural way into their informal 'out of role' conversation and interaction. This takes place in an atmosphere of heightened language awareness in which not only the student but also the teacher chooses his or her words with care: not an unusual situation in *any* training or professional context. For *all* professions, arts and sciences teach their particular specialised *languages* to their students, and train them in communicating and using this language in their jobs. A chemistry student must know what 'calcium chloride' refers to, and an engineer must know in his own language what a technical instruction means.

We *use* language to *teach* language. That is the paradox of teaching languages. In one-to-one teaching where special purpose language training is often the demand, we can even *use* the student's specialised language to draw parallels with the skills we as language teachers are sharing. Sell words to the salesman. Demonstrate language flowcharts and 'software' to the programmer. Teach the auditor to audit the language of his own reports, build models of language for the engineer, get the artist to draw sounds, use graphs with the economist or businessman and grammar equations with the mathematician.

Creative drilling and skilling can take all these forms and more, tailored to the knowledge and type of skill already possessed by the student, and using his or her speciality as a *model* and *metaphor* for language and communication.

Authenticity

Inauthentic teaching forces students to speak without *saying* anything. Even the most superficially 'communicative' exercises can involve students in inauthentic speaking. The artificiality of a lot of role-play for example, is well-known. By contrast, experience shows that even something as mechanical-seeming as a drill need not be inauthentic at all. A lot can be *said* by variations in tone and stress.

Similarly there is nothing inauthentic about teacher and student talking *about* language in a lesson: for the student, nothing could be more natural. The joint focus on language forms and functions on the part of teacher and student, and the transmission of the teacher's skills to the student represent the basic 'role-play' between them. How authentic *other* role-plays are depends on how authentically the student and the teacher can carry them off, and their relevance to the student's needs.

Learning and listening skills go hand in hand. Students can neither study nor acquire new language unless they can identify the spoken words and register these mentally and/or in writing. On the other hand, you will find that students only hear and see words which they expect to hear and see. Student deafness to words, particularly 'function' words, eg articles, prepositions, some pronouns, as opposed to content-carrying words, may be due to the speaker's use of contractions or the liaisons of natural speech. However this is itself an example of the fact that the student lacks appropriate search-images and expectations. Instead students' search-images are based either on L1 or on *word* images of L2. But spoken language is full of 'nonsense' syllables created by liaison, weak forms and contraction which the student will not recognise or register. Students must be trained to distil the words from the sound, to recognise not only the 'official' words of the written language but the 'unofficial' ones of the spoken language. The written language is sequenced in words; the spoken in sound-syllables.

Comparing their own transcript of a tape or dictation with the complete or original text is a valuable way of making students aware of what they are *not* hearing. In this way they become more aware of the words they are deaf to, or the sounds they are failing to discriminate. Such an exercise is not necessarily 'communicative'. It does not assume or require that the student needs to be able to take dictation or transcribe material in real life. And yet it exercises a mental skill, a micro-skill, that is indispensible for listening and learning. The student does not 'practise' listening. He or she learns to listen, to correct his or her search-images.

The same thing can be said of reading. Students will literally be *blind* to words on the page that they do not expect or which do not fit into their internal model of language. They can be taught to see these words (usually function words again) by comparing their own recording or dictation to teacher of a written text with the original. In this case the teacher must faithfully follow the spoken word of the student, or rather, follow the student's omission of words. Again, we are not assuming that the student necessarily needs to record or dictate from text in real life.

The skill that is exercised is a micro-skill, though if this can be practised as an 'authentic listening task', so much the better.

The important thing in traditional listening tasks, however, is invariably content rather than sound, form and 'function' words. It is the big words rather than the small ones, the content rather than the form. The type of listening needed for *language learning* rather than information processing is quite different. Getting the student to focus on form as well as content, to 'audit' and really *hear* rather than listen in the normal way requires special methods, and can be vital in registering meaning properly too:

> *The temperature dropped to two degrees.*
> *The temperature dropped by two degrees.*

Here, as in many examples, the small words do count!

Biographical content

'Authentic material' is material which says something, which speaks from the person. Teachers have a habit of hiding behind exercises, of giving exercises instead of themselves. We associate 'talks' with an impersonal, didactic sort of lecturing when in fact both informal talks and lectures provide a wonderful medium for the person to show himself or herself, to tell his or her story.

One-to-one of course provides an ideal context for the sharing of biographical material and stories. We should not be surprised if many, if not all, of our students are rich in such material and find great satisfaction in sharing it. The telling of stories from one's personal experience and history is a conversational art and skill that many students also take for granted in their mother tongue and which corresponds to their very understanding of the word 'conversation'. Conversation is not just 'small talk' to kill time or show 'polite' interest. It is a *format* which *naturally* and *authentically* employs the widest range of language one could wish for.

Nor need the sharing of biographical material be limited to the student. This sort of 'teacher talking time', in which the teacher is actually saying something, and giving something of him- or herself is far more likely to engage the interest and attention of the student than anything else, and can be practised as an art by the teacher for suggestive, dramatic and pedagogic effect.

Authentic communication as a principle in one-to-one teaching would mean very little without biographical content.

For this it is useful to have on hand a wide range of topics for talks which can bring up the widest variety of biographical material, including also material from the student's professional life. Remember also that such talks are not just monologues but may involve the narration of dialogues as well as growing as a dialogue between teacher and student. A list of suggested topics is given on the following page.

A basic working paradigm

Suggested topics for biographical talks

My best learning experience
My first job
My last job
My secret ambition
My best friend
My worst accident
My worst illness
My greatest regret
My proudest achievement
My hopes for the next 5 years
My greatest disappointment
My strongest belief
My most important decision
My job and what I like about it
My city/town/village and what I
like about it
My country and what I like about it
My closest call with death
My biggest business risk
My biggest inspiration
My most memorable dream

The worst job I ever had
The most important lesson life has
taught me
The longest minute I ever spent
The best year of my life
The strangest person I ever met
The most interesting person I ever
met
The most courageous act I ever
witnessed
The biggest crisis of my life
The person I admire most
The greatest help I ever received
The thing that interests me most in
people
The strangest coincidence in my
life

How I have changed
How I reached my present
position
How my company started
How I overcame a habit
How I overcame a weakness
How I overcame a fear
How one idea increased my
happiness

The last time I had a flat tyre

The last time I fell in love
The last time I felt envy
The last time I got angry
The last time I got drunk
The last time I spoke English
(before this course)
The last time I was in pain
The last time I remembered a dream
The last time I was terrified

Why I am not religious
Why I am not an atheist
Why I smoke
Why I vote the way I do

If I lived again . . .
If I had a past life . . .
If I had the chance . . .
If I had the courage . . .
If I had the power . . .
If I had the skill . . .

The three most vivid scenes I
recall from my life
The three most important people
in my life
The three most important men/
women in my life
The three most important
principles I follow
The three most important qualities
for someone in my position

A secret I am prepared to reveal
about myself
A book that influenced me for life
A person that influenced me for
life
An event that influenced me for life

A place I would love to visit again
A person I would love to meet
again
An era I would like to have lived in

Something I will never do again
Something I often dream about

What I hope my children will learn
from me
What I do with the most confidence
What I hope to achieve this year

Re-formulation

Re-formulation is a variety of procedures in which the teacher provides a format for student input and then provides the language
that the student lacked in expressing him- or herself. The student
provides the content expressed in inadequate form. The teacher reformulates, that is to say provides the missing forms. Reformulation can be done orally, on the board, or in writing; during,
or between, lessons. The initial input may take the form of a
student draft, presentation, or structured or unstructured conversation. All student input, whether structured or not, reveals 'covert
error', occasioned by lack of knowledge of relevant language forms.
Re-formulation provides these forms. In auditing this resulting text
students can identify these for themselves.

As a tool reformulation avoids specific dangers:
- haphazard and ineffective 'spot' correction.
- doing work which tests without teaching.
- teaching which teaches the student his job;
  teaches him *what* to say instead of *how* to say it.
- teaching language tangential or irrelevant to the **individual**
  student's needs.

Community Language Learning (CLL) is a technique where students
say whatever they wish in L1 and the teacher then whispers the L2
version to the student, who practises and repeats it, recording the L2
version for subsequent use. The *content* is dictated by the student, the
form only by the teacher, in contrast to most language learning where the
student has little or no control over the content.

The basic principle of CLL can be applied without the student having
to use L1. If the student feels able to communicate his or her message
without resorting to L1 all the better. Then, instead of either making
piecemeal corrections *or* interpreting for the student the teacher has the
opportunity to reformulate the student's message in appropriate language
and at a level just above that demonstrated by the student.

CLL is one version of the reformulation principle. I say 'principle'
rather than simply 'technique' because it is the essence of a wide range of
activities performed by both teacher and student. Even a transformation
drill is an example of reformulation, in this case, performed by the
student. Language learning as such is *about* reformulation: in selecting
language to teach we are hoping to provide our student with useful
'forms' or 'containers' by which he or she can re-present, and reformulate, a message in different words.

One-to-one teaching in particular offers ideal opportunities for
applying the principle of reformulation in a more direct way including:

- Oral reformulation L1/L2 to L2
- Reformulation in writing (eg from dictation by student)
- Retrospective reformulation

The advantages of this approach are many:
- The teacher fulfils the role of someone there to *provide* language for
  the student to use.

- This language is tailored to the student's needs and personal idiom. Most students do have opinions about the language they are learning—words they like or dislike; expressions with which they feel comfortable. Here they can be offered choices and involved in the selection of language for themselves.

- The student makes his or her own objective comparison of the original and reformulated language.

- The recording spoken by the student is clean and relatively error free.

- When the student compares his or her own script with a transcript of the recording this is more than just 'self-correction'. The teacher's choice of language in reformulating student utterances is more than just corrective. It is a form of *presentation* of language.

- The student begins with the whole: the transcript of a recorded presentation/dialogue/role play and then examines the parts, in context already.

- It is the student's task to identify and sort the language contained in the text.

- The vocabulary, structures and functions it contains will present a range of language choices eg different ways of suggesting something, or different ways of talking about the past ... but ...

- It is up to the student to decide which of this language is new or useful. Even though the language may not be unfamiliar, it may still not be language that the student **uses**. In this way reformulation is an aid to **conscious language acquisition.** It is not a question of learning new language or of just knowing 'old' language, but of the student becoming conscious of the usefulness of language that was already passively known or understood.

- Tailoring the suit to the customer. Where there is a range of linguistic choices present in the text, these should be listed and left to the student to choose from according to taste and comfort, eg choosing from a list of expressions for a given function those which the student feels most at home using.

- This language extraction work does not need to be followed by transfer and personalisation to fit the student's own needs or job situation. This work has already been done.

- Instead it can be followed up by further speechwork: auditing features of pronunciation and/or recording repetition drills for the student to practise with alone, using the tape recorder as a mini-lab.

Retrospective reformulation

With advanced or highly fluent students it may not always be appropriate or necessary to correct or reformulate their utterances at every turn. If a student speaks with interest and for a relatively long time on a certain subject, it would be counter-productive to interrupt this fluency. Instead the teacher can monitor the student's language silently and reformulate with greater precision and economy of speech when the lesson is over. The reformulated language can be presented to the student in the form of a reformulated transcript or summary.

An example of a reformulated role play, recorded by a student on his first day is given below.

Reformulation and role play

The teacher can combine the job of reformulation with participation with the student in a role play. In this case there are several alternatives:

- Student takes both roles and teacher reformulates.
- Student takes one role but suggests or anticipates language for both. Teacher reformulates language for both roles but records one role in his or her own voice.
- As above but with the teacher improvising the other role and reformulating only student turns.

Here is a short extract from a re-formulated role play recorded by a student on his first day. 'Clearview' are manufacturers of spectacle frames.
Scene: The Clearview Stand at the Trade Exhibition, Milan. Teacher in role of Clearview Rep.

Ah, Mr Solomon. How nice to see you again.

Thank you. I see you have a nice stand this year.

Well, we do our best. And how are things going in Spain?

Oh, not too badly thank you. But it's always a pleasure to come to Italy.

Have you had a chance to inspect our new range yet?

No, not yet. But I've been looking forward to it. But I'm forgetting my manners. Let me introduce you to . . .

How do you do.

Pleased to meet you, though if I'm not mistaken we HAVE met before. In Frankfurt I believe.

Oh of course, do excuse me. At that time you were with Mr. . . . , weren't you.

That's right.

Anyway, why don't we make ourselves comfortable and have a glass of this delightful wine?

That sounds all right to me.

And how about you Mr Solomon?

It IS tempting, but if you don't mind I'll stick to coffee for the moment.

A basic working paradigm

Fine. But perhaps I can interest you in some of our new models. Let's start with this one. It belongs to our new men's range, with features I'm sure you'll appreciate. I should add that we've also taken note of your calibre requirements and adjusted the frame measurements accordingly.

May I?

Oh please do.

Contrast this role play dialogue with the transcript of another student addressing the teacher on Day 1:

> I have .. er .. Steve//what I have to say is//if I would like to ask//
> if you are allowed//when I smoke and he said//I have to question
> 'Do you mind if I smoke?'
> Is that correct?//OK then I have ordered correct.
> . . .'I don't mind at all'. . .'I don't//MIND AT ALL?!' 'I don't mind
> at all'?
> OK that's .. er .. Ja, Ja.
> 'I discuss with Jill and Brian this morning about the discussion . . .
> the debate,
> 'deBATE?', 'deBATE'? DE . . . deBATE in England about . . .
>   I don't think if you//'came familiar'?//with George Falk.
> Is that correct?//No, 'came familiar' is not correct.

Here the student clearly feels himself to be talking to Teacher. His desire to check out his communicative competence with the teacher interferes with communicative performance, and quite unnecessarily so. For he demonstrates in this performance that he knows what is right and wrong without the help of the teacher.

In a large number of cases mature adult students are reduced to this sort of stammering not because they are incompetent or because they are subject to constant correction by the teacher, but because they are performing in front of a teacher and they **want** to be corrected.

What is more, this stammering discourse is contagious. Even teachers catch it. For how is the teacher to respond, in a natural and human way, except by responding to the student's desire for correction and thus colluding with the essentially unhelpful game of 'watch your mouth'.

The student's desire for correction comes from a *desire* for accurate communicative *performance,* and yet it interferes with this performance.

The discourse *of* the student is distorted by the *role* of 'student', by the effect of the *belief* that:

- everything counts except the present moment
- that teaching is a preparation for future performance
- that communicative competence is more important than communicative performance.

The distortion of the student's discourse by this unnecessary self-interruption and self-correction can be prevented using reformulation, at the same time helping the student realise his or her true goal of fluent *performance.*

Reformulation combines presentation of language with remedial work and correction. Used in combination with role play it provides a structured format for altering the 'language game' between teacher and student so as to encourage rather than threaten student confidence.

Double reformulation

This combines retrospective reformulation and role-reformulation. It is a retrospective reformulation performed out of lesson hours on the transcript of a role play eg rewriting in a different register, or including more specialised language than was available to the teacher during the initial 'run'. Often the initial role play serves mainly to highlight language needs that cannot be met impromptu, but *can* be met and realised in proper context by retrospective reformulation.

Reformulation and boardwork

The student's initial draft of written work can be done on the board instead of on paper. Alternatively the teacher can use the board to present reformulations of student input before they are either written down or recorded by the student. This has the benefit of allowing clear presentation of language structures and language choices available to the student, who can then choose between alternatives. In most cases I find that students have an excellent 'ear' for the language most appropriate for their needs and appreciate the opportunity both to see this language on the board and to choose from a range of different expressions.

If the teacher is reformulating for the student to record orally it need not be considered bad practice for the written language to be seen in advance. To avoid this becoming *mere* reading aloud a number of devices can be adopted:

- the student can be asked to re-dictate the written words or write them on the board having heard the utterance spoken by the teacher.
- the teacher can progressively de-construct written work by wiping away words or segments of the sentence for the student to recall and practise orally.
- the boardwork can (and should) be marked phonetically to highlight important features of pronunciation in preparation for oral practice and recording.
- the student can be asked simply not to *look* at the board while he or she speaks (and then to check his or her language and pronunciation against the phonetically marked writing) before recording.

Board reformulation is an encouragement to student participation in the reformulation process and the activation of passive knowledge.

Student reformulation

Until now we have considered the teacher as reformulator. But the aim of teaching is to improve the student's skill in appropriately and correctly reformulating his or her own output.

For this it is useful for the student to record his or her own unreformulated words on tape or in writing; students can be asked to monitor for errors and make corrections or suggest alternative language. The teacher can also chip in with suggestions, corrections and questions. Having made notes on all the relevant points the student will then be in a position to give it a second go, and reformulate the original letter or presentation independently.

It is important that the language notes relevant to this reformulation be recorded separately so that the student works them into it in revising or re-recording. One way of ensuring that the *student* practises reformulation autonomously is to ask him or her to reconstruct and repeat the initial writing or speaking task from these notes alone.

Reconstruction

The reconstruction and re-presentation or summary of a text from key words and/or language notes is an excellent exercise in itself. If an authentic text is being used it is important to first get the student to identify the lexis and language which is new to him or her. There is no point in a student paraphrasing a text containing new and useful language with language that is old, improvised and clumsy. The point is not for the student to say the same thing in *other* words but to learn from the text or tape and use the language it offers. It can never be repeated too often that what is important for the student is not the word or phrase that he or she didn't know before, but the word or phrase that the student *understands* but *doesn't make use* of. The most valuable 'micro-skill' a student can learn is to register and *pick up* language that others use but he or she doesn't; to *learn to acquire.*

The importance of collocations, for example, is not just that the student understand them but that he or she should employ them in place of uncommon and improvised combinations of words, particularly in the area of business language, but also on the level of everyday idiom, phrasal verbs etc.

Read a text, or play a recording and ask the student to stop you, or stop the tape, whenever he or she hears words or phrases that are useful. Alternatively ask the student to note language in a table with headings such as the following:

Words or phrases I don't understand	Words or phrases that I understand but don't use	Words or phrases that I want to use

Re-formatting and Reformulation

The sample sheets that follow (pages 39–41) are all examples of oral or written input from the student reformulated via boardwork. In addition however they were 'retrospectively' reformatted by the teacher.

Reformatting is a basic device employed in all EFL textbooks. It includes information-transfer type exercises, for example, in which the student completes tables or graphs from reading or listening, or conversely, verbalises the information they contain, ('Table to talk').

Initial Format	Re-formatting	Final Format
Text		Talk
Tape	→ Task →	Table
Table		Tape
Talk		Text

This scheme can itself be shown in the form of a table; an example of each type of possible follow-up work on reformulation is given.

To From	TEXT	TAPE	TABLE
TEXT	Typing out with language notes	Re-recording dialogue from text	Extracting and sorting key information or key lexis from reading
TAPE	Transcription or aural gap-filling	Copying a tape with new format such as open dialogue or drill	As above, from listening
TABLE	Reconstruction in writing from table of information	Oral reconstruction or role play from table of information	Re-sorting or resequencing lexis or information

Other possibilities include:

- transferring key lexis and language points to a set of cards.
- rewriting in a different medium and/or register.
- text-to-talk eg role-play discussion of a memo/letter/article.
- text-to-telephone call.
- preparing revision sheets for lexis and structures used in the reformulation, providing a key for the student in the margin.
- The collocation dictionary. This is an excellent format for the student to use in recording lexis on a *two- or three-word level* rather than the usual *one-word* level. All the student needs is a standard index book or alphabetic dividers for a file.

Let us say that the student finds the collocation *to enter the market* in a text. This will be recorded under **E** for *enter* along with a selection of other nouns that commonly follow this verb:

> **to enter   a market**
> **a room**
> **(into) negotiations**
> **a figure**

A basic working paradigm

The student can also enter under **M** for *market* all the verbs that commonly precede this noun, for example:

	enter	
	penetrate	
	research	
to	**discover**	**a market**
	exploit	
	expand	

In addition, the nominal form of the verb and the verbal form of the noun can be entered under their respective first letters. For example, also under **M**:

to market	**a product**
	a service
	a design

Adjectival and participle forms can also be recorded:

competitive	**marketing**
	market

marketing	**manager**
	strategy

The point is to record words that are commonly used together, and to record them in their different family variations. This is especially important where a given verb, say, may take different prepositions; for prepositional and phrasal verbs, or where either the nominal or the verbal form of a word is lacking in the student's L1.

It is not necessary to record all possible word permutations at one time. But the collocation dictionary allows the student to accumulate his or her own lexical capital by providing an explicit format for this.

Summary

It is perhaps useful to provide a summary of the basic paradigm that I am proposing for the one-to-one situation:

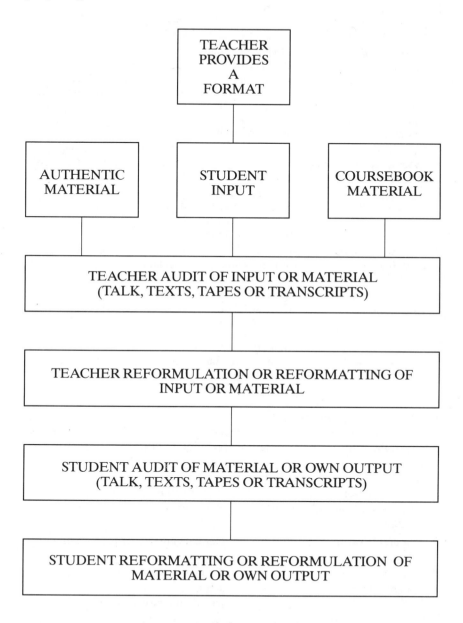

This material may be expanded somewhat into a "basic course programme", which diverges considerably from many of the timetables presented to one-to-one students or course organisers.

It will, I hope, be noted that this programme contains as intrinsic to it, strong elements of student-input and teacher-flexibility. It is designed to evolve as the course itself develops. It incorporates all the central ideas discussed in this chapter.

A basic working paradigm

		What?	How?	Why?
1.	Student input	–situations –interlocutors –skills	registration form and interview	communicative needs analysis
2.	Student input (*formatted* to meet comm. needs)	–report –presentation –role play	writing speaking L1/L2	raw material
3.	Teacher *audits* student input	–missing vocabulary –missing structures –missing functions	cohesion pronunciation	linguistic needs-analysis
4.	Teacher *reformulates and reformats* and feeds in new language	–orally –in writing –on board in discussion with	immediate or retrospective	determination of extra input requirements
5.	Student audits and re-formats, reformulated text, tape, transcript	–new vocabulary structures, functions	cohesion and pronunciation	learning requirements
6.	Additional *Teacher* input	–authentic material –coursebook mat. –drills and teacher prepared material	all 4 skills	language practice
7.	Student *reformulates* his or her own output	–rewriting –re-presentation –re-enactment	writing speaking L2	testing
8.	*Reinforcement* and follow-up	–rewriting –cloze dictation –speechwork and presentation training –collation and filing of coursework	memorisation	final product

Finally it is perhaps helpful to give an example of auditing skills in action, in the form of a specific teaching sequence. This is discussed much more fully in the chapter on techniques appropriate for one-to-one.

	Teacher	**Student**
1.	Reads a text aloud in short segments	Repeats
2.	Corrects pronunciation if necessary	Repeats and records the segment
3.	Re-plays recording in short segments	Transcribes recording in short segments (or dictates for teacher to type)
4.	Teacher and student work on making the text cohesive and coherent by:	

–guessing words to fill any gaps in the transcription

–inserting punctuation left out in the transcription

–correcting mistakes in the transcription through attention to grammatical error and inconsistencies or lexical inappropriateness

–appropriate paragraphing

5. Teacher reads text again	Student fills gaps according to text and corrects spelling, punctuation and paragraphing mistakes
6. Teacher reads text again	Student marks liaisons, syllable stress and intonation (eg high rise and low termination), or marks occurrences of a particular vowel or consonant.
7. Teacher asks student to identify instances of particular language sounds, structures or functions.	Student scans text

8. Teacher and student discuss register, structures and intonation in relation to the content and context of the text.

9. Teacher models intonation, or transformation of text into another register or person (eg third to first person)	Student re-records the text in a different register/tense/person

10. Contrastive comparison of initial and final transcripts and/or recordings.

Reformulation in Action

Example of a one-week intensive course (3 hrs/day) using reformulation techniques as the basic method. (Pre-course preparation: none)

Day 1 Student asked to give a presentation of his company. After each 'chunk' of input from student, teacher reformulated and student wrote down the sentences dictated by teacher. The procedure was broken up by intermittent questioning from teacher and vocabulary work on board. Took the full 3 hrs. (The presentation is given in its final form on page 39).

Day 2 Student dictated reformulated presentation for teacher to type. Student then asked to go through presentation thinking of possible questions from his audience and answering these.
Teacher reformulated each question and answer for student to repeat and then immediately record. Student then transcribed the complete dialogue from his walkman and without help from teacher. After this he dictated the transcription to teacher for typing. As I typed I substituted alternative 'functional' expressions and corrected a couple of small errors (articles).
Student then compared my transcript with his, and marked the typed transcript for word stress, sentence stress and liaison.

Day 3 a. Review of presentation from Day 1 with student marking text with highlighters. Focus on identifying verb forms used, the use of articles in contrast with French, prepositions and present participles. Student made language notes.

b. Teacher provided typed format for a formal speech of welcome (see page 40) relevant to student needs, and composed of sentence heads.
Student asked to complete sentences to create a speech for use with his own clients. Teacher reformulated his suggestions and

provided alternative language options for student to choose from. Final speech dictated by student to teacher for typing. Student asked to mark *keywords* in speech and reproduce it from these. Student's first attempt at reproduction recorded. This made him aware that the *important* keywords are not the *content* words but the 'function' words and unfamiliar formal structures. Student then marked a new set of keywords, ie those he had failed to remember in attempting to reproduce the speech. Speech then practised 3 times by 'auto-prompting':

1. student scans a line of the text until he feels familiar with it
2. student looks up and silently recalls the line
3. student speaks the line as if to a real audience

At every 'go' the number of errors made by the student dropped. At the third go only one minor omission. The *second* stage in this procedure is the most important and effective. This needs emphasising.

Student then presented the speech from the 'functional' keywords alone, including those omitted in the auto-prompt rehearsals. This was successful. Finally teacher pointed out contrast of 'high-rise' and 'low-termination' stresses, and encouraged student to speak each line in one breath with liaison and low-termination on the last content word.

Day 4 a. Gap-filling exercise using text of student's company presentation.

Blacked-out words or phrases selected according to language novel to this particular student.

b. Further practice of speech of welcome from Day 3.

c. Reading of authentic article from a relevant specialised journal chosen to stimulate student input.

Article worked on paragraph by paragraph with the following procedure:
—Auditing for collocations and useful phrases
—Student summarised each paragraph in one sentence using new language *from* the text.
—Student expressed his opinion on the points stated in the paragraph with teacher reformulating and providing functional language for expressing views and reactions.

Student then dictated the complete list of collocations and functional expressions to teacher for typing. Student asked to dictate some of the functions syllable-by-syllable, for language awareness and pronunciation practice, particularly of liaison.

Day 5 Re-recording of all reformulated material on cassette for student to take away. Collation of transcripts in hard-bound book of document wallets.

1. Student presentation. Recorded by teacher.

2. Question and answer dialogue on presentation. Recorded as an 'open dialogue' with gaps between question and answer for the student to anticipate the latter.

3. Speech of welcome, recorded by student.

4. Functional expressions. Each recorded twice with intervals for the student to silently repeat.

5. Collocations of verb and object. Recorded by teacher as a series of prompts (eg object-nouns) with interval for student to recall appropriate possible verbs going with the noun, or vice versa. For example:

> *to sit in on . . .*
> *(interval)*
> *to sit in on a discussion*
> *requirements*
> *(interval)*
> *to meet requirements*

(Since most cassette players have pause buttons the intervals are optional except for use while driving.)

Example of a student presentation in final form

We are a Belgian company specialising in the provision of technical training, support and assistance for foreign air forces. The company was founded in 1984 following a decision by the MOD that such services could best be provided by an independent company employing its own specialised staff.

Since 1984 Webbair has successfully fulfilled contracts with more than ten countries around the world either directly or in partnership with French manufacturers.

Our training services cover the full range of systems usually employed by air forces, except helicopters. This includes: planes, engines, tactical missiles, on-board radar, ground radar, electronic equipment, communications and so on.

All Webbair's work is undertaken only with the full authority of the Belgian government and under the direct supervision of the Belgian air force.

We work in close cooperation with all major Belgian manufacturers. We can provide both theoretical and on-job training for small groups, large groups, and if necessary, individuals.

Before any contract is agreed we undertake a thorough analysis of our client's training requirements. This includes defining the syllabus, planning the programme, preparing materials, and establishing trainee prerequisites. All this is done in close consultation with clients and manufacturers.

Courses may be conducted in Belgium and/or the client's home country. Training is given by highly qualified and experienced personnel . . . ex-military or professional, and geared to the client's equipment.

Our training package can include all necessary language

instruction for trainers and trainees or the use of technical interpreters and translators.

Although Webbair is a young company, our personnel can provide you with the benefit of years of experience.

(The only change from the original piece of student work is that I have altered one or two names and factual details for obvious reasons.)

Example of 'question & answer' session based on presentation

Why were there no companies like Webbair before 1984?

Before 1984 Belgian manufacturers provided their own assistance and if necessary the Belgian air force provided additional training.

Do you have any competitors in Belgium or abroad?

Many companies like Webbair have been created in countries selling armaments. In Belgium we don't have any competitors but we do have partners.

How competitive are your prices?

If the Belgian government offered you free training Webbair couldn't compete, but Webbair prices compare well with those of foreign companies.

Example of 'welcome speech' discussed above

Gentlemen, I am very glad to welcome you to Paris.
First of all, because we are looking forward to working together closely.
And secondly, because I've had the pleasure of getting to know some of you personally and it's always nice to meet old friends. I should like to wish you a pleasant stay in Paris and say that we at Webbair, in particular Mr X, will do our best to help you find your feet. I hope that your stay and our discussions will bring positive benefits for both parties, and trust that your visit to the electronics school will prove satisfactory.
Now, I'm no longer going to stand between you and these refreshments . . . and I should like to propose a toast to both our countries.

Sample of phrases and collocations collected by student after reformulation

I think it's an excellent idea.
That sounds like a good idea.
What a good idea.

That's journalistic exaggeration.
It's a bit exaggerated, don't you think?

If that's the case, why . . . ?

He's got a point.
I think they've got a point, don't you?

Its rather misleading.

The aerospace industry should not decide either.

to pursue an aim

to take part in discussions
to remain in discussion
to sit in on discussions
to prejudice discussions

to cut costs
to yield savings/interest/profits
to economise on maintenance/staff/materials
to save time/money
to spend time/money
to state categorically
to meet requirements
to show interest in something
to enjoy a view
to repudiate a view
to draw conclusions
to exert an influence/effect
to make a decision on the basis of . . .
to expand/diminish prospects
("evaporating prospects")

A basic working paradigm

Basic Flow Chart of Reformulation Options

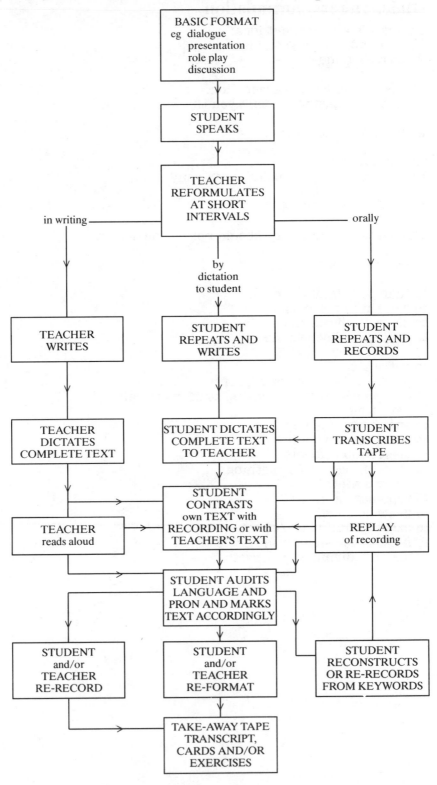

Reformulation for beginners

Particularly for beginners on short intensive courses, a step-by-step structural approach cannot be recommended. Beginners are more interested in content rather than 'function' words, in the lexis rather than the ligaments of language. At the same time there is the danger of one-to-one being a somewhat isolating experience for teacher and student if the latter does not, at a very early stage, experience the satisfaction of genuine self-expression in L2. Helping the student to do this makes the teaching more interesting and rewarding for the teacher as well.

From this point of view reformulation offers an excellent means for the student to dive straight into meaningful use of L2 without weeks of more-or-less abstract pre-teaching. If he or she is really a total beginner we must reformulate from L1. The teacher interprets, and the result is a taped dialogue or presentation in which the student is using the target language throughout. With this at hand, 'post-teaching' can begin. The student can be asked to transcribe the recording and the transcription exploited as a text which is both authentic and personalised.

Naturally we will not wish to 'feed' the student with language which is too sophisticated. Our aim in reformulation is not to provide a word-for-word translation of every student utterance but to literally *interpret* what he or she wishes to *say* in the simplest and most useful words possible. This being so, our own understanding of the student's mother tongue need not be anything more than primitive for us to 'get the message'. The student's own appreciation of our limits in understanding will prompt him or her to use 'caretaker' language with us, and the result may well be a dialogue in which single-word utterances by the student (in L2 as well as L1) are exchanged for well-formed sentences provided by the teacher.

Non-verbal aids to communication will certainly count a lot (gesture, pointing, mime) and contribute to a communicative exchange of a sort which is entirely authentic, spontaneous, and natural. The difference is only the in-built bias by which this natural 'language exchange' is geared to the profit of *one* of the foreign language speakers: the student. It is the student's input, rather than the teacher's that reformulation is designed to make space for, and offer suitable vehicles of articulation. On the other hand the teacher's input (in the form of questions or short responses) may well form an integral and useful part of the dialogue recording that is built up. This could also permit a 'role-reversal' recording in which the teacher takes the student's part and once again models the language used in the original dialogue.

3. The teacher

Teaching is about techniques, but more fundamentally it is about attitudes. This is true above all in the essentially personal situation of one-to-one teaching.

No amount of 'technique', good material or careful preparation of the classtime will help if the one-to-one teacher has not prepared him- or herself. It is the teacher's attitudes, and the way they manifest themselves to the student, which are probably the single most important influence on the success or failure of the teaching. The reader is invited to consider some of his or her own attitudes on the following pages.

The role of the teacher

Unfortunately the very word 'teacher' tends to suggest a classroom, and with this the demands of classroom management. It is through effective classroom management that the teacher remains 'one-up', 'in control', or however this idea is described. This is true whether the approach taken is teacher- or learner-centred. The class teacher tries to be aware of the differing needs and problems of students, but cannot allow any one student's needs to dominate the class.

How different a situation in one-to-one! Here it is precisely this one student's needs, personality and psychology that are paramount. The student may actually be a manager or managing director. This is important, for whilst student expectations of the role of the teacher may be as biased by the classroom and by school as the teacher's, the professional world of the student is not the world of the classroom. It is far more likely to be a world in which the student is 'one-up' or on his or her way up.

For the student, as well as for the teacher, who will wish to encourage self-responsibility, it is to the roles and relationships that govern the student's professional world that we should look in finding models for the role of the teacher in one-to-one. One-to-one interaction, 'face-to-face' is a part of business and professional life. In particular it is in the service professions that we can find parallels with the job of the one-to-one teacher.

Diagnosis, resource management, consultancy; assistant, informer, partner, auditor, secretary, copywriter, analyst. These are some of the terms that come to mind to describe real functions of the teacher . . . as well as coach, trainer, tutor, instructor, and other words more reminiscent of the world of school.

The target language

Anyone putting their skills at the service of a client begins in a one-down position. In the case of the teacher doing one-to-one we start with a massive information gap. Who is this person? What is his or her job? What is his or her motivation and purpose? What is he or she like? To moderate this gap we may or may not have available one or more of the following:

- a booking or application form
- a needs-analysis questionnaire
- a test
- a self-evaluation and statement of needs
- a briefing from another teacher or Director of Studies
- information from a student's colleague or friend
- the benefit of a prior interview

Teachers tend to agree that whilst all these are important in principle, not so in practice. They frequently say "You don't really know the student till you've met them". This is one good reason for an interview. But even an interview cannot tell us the most important thing of all, namely what the student's language is. Yet if we are teaching English for Profesional Purposes, for Business Purposes, Specific Purposes . . . for Individual Purposes, this is crucial.

I enjoy one-to-one for the opportunity it provides to serve another person and at the same time to learn his or her language. By this I do not mean L1 but the student's whole 'existential' language as expressed in a field of work, a way of speaking, even a way of living. I believe that, on one level, all communication involves learning each other's language in this sense. That is one of its purposes.

The one-to-one 'studio', though it contains only teacher and student is perhaps the most overcrowded classroom of them all.

This is especially true for short-intensive courses with a large number of continuous contact hours. Once again, where else but in language schools are individuals who have never met before and who may have very little in common expected to spend a major part of each working day together in a confined space? Even secretaries or business partners are not obliged to work together continuously in this way.

So the starting situation is quite abnormal by most everyday standards, and may even be aggravated by teacher and student having to spend lunchtimes, evenings or weekends together.

Extensive one-to-one does not share this problem but nor does it escape the danger that with only two people in the room they each may feel their own boundaries threatened, and feel the space of operations, usually a small room, to be confining.

Despite the best of intentions and an amiable relationship the challenge is to avoid this tendency to withdrawal and contraction of teacher and student in on themselves. This tendency may even be increased by well-meaning attempts to bring students 'out of themselves'.

This is just another way of pointing out that in classes the students have the support and stimulus of a group or can use it as a shelter. It also highlights the central problem in developing an approach to one-to-one teaching: *creating space* for learning.

Space can mean many things here, not least space in one's own mind, uncluttered by preconceptions and lesson plans. It also means space for attention to the student and responding to his or her signals.

There is space for silence, for responding with consideration rather than reacting automatically. And respect for SST, 'student silent time'.

This implies also allotting a space-time—for the student to work alone. 'Work' here can mean writing. It can also mean the student doing pronunciation work, drills or work with a recorder. The teacher may leave the room (yes, it is permissible) or remove his or her presence to another corner or another activity. This is not always an easy freedom to grant oneself. After all, one is being paid, and probably by the hour. Nevertheless there will be times when it is not only appropriate but highly beneficial. Removing the aura of supervision is one way of giving the student the feeling that he or she has time. By passing the management of this time to the student we also call forth his or her independent and self-willed learning activity. This is itself an exercise for the student, and a valuable one.

The opposite of this is pushing too hard, stifling the student. Teachers can also push themselves too hard. Feeling one-to-one to be a no-exit situation, and reacting to what we believe to be the student's expectation for us to 'perform' as teachers is a great danger. The result is often that the only way out appears to be to fill the threatening space with talk, input or activity. Very soon there is no room to breathe, the student feels pushed, and tiredness sets in.

Noticing physical restlessness in ourselves or our student is also a signal for a change of pace, activity or medium. A signal perhaps to do things standing up, to increase vocal energy, to call a break or to re-arrange the space.

Changing rooms may not be possible. Rearranging the furniture and seating is. The restlessness on the other hand, may be one-sided. If it is the teacher who feels the impulse to get up and move around there is nothing that glues us to a chair. Demonstrating ease of mobility is a way of relaxing students and helping them not to feel constrained.

What is your basic attitude to one-to-one teaching? Which of these two images is closer to your idea?

> HIGH STUDENT EXPECTATIONS GIVING VALUE FOR MONEY PRESSURE HEADACHE LONG CONTACT HOURS NO EXIT CONFINEMENT TENSION ANXIETY TIREDNESS WHAT A BORE WHAT'S THE TIME MY, WE GOT THROUGH THAT QUICKLY ALL GO INTENSIVE EXECUTIVE HIGH-COST PRESTIGE HE EARNS A LOT PROBABLY GOT A MERCEDES WHEN WAS THE LAST TIME I HAD A HOLIDAY CONSTANT BALANCING TRICK SMILE WHILE I THINK WHAT TO DO NEXT TO FILL THE TIME ISN'T IT TIME FOR NO I DON'T THINK I COULD STAND ANOTHER COFFEE AND I'LL HAVE TO SIT THROUGH ANOTHER LUNCH ETC MAKING POLITE NOISES AND BEING A LIVING DICTIONARY HOW DID I GET INTO THIS JOB ANYWAY BUT I'D BETTER GET RESULTS OR ELSE.... THIS CHAIR REALLY IS UNCOMFORTABLE.

Teacher attitudes to one-to-one

There are experienced teachers and teacher trainers who regard one-to-one as a boring and exhausting waste of time.

It is useful and important to check out your own beliefs by putting yourself in the student's shoes.

Ask yourself these questions. You do not need to answer them straight off, but give yourself time and bear them in mind.

- How would you go about learning a foreign language from scratch or improving your knowledge and skill in one you have some familiarity with?

- Would you consider being taught in this way?

- If so, why?

- If not, why not?

- What do you believe about one-to-one teaching?

- Would you seek tuition on:
      an extensive basis (eg one or two hours a week)
      an intensive basis (eg seven hours a day)
      as a long-term or short-term supplement to:
          an intensive group course
          an extensive group course
          an intensive one-to-one course

- What sort of teacher would you want:
      native or non-native?
      same sex or opposite sex?
      trained or untrained?
      traditional or modern?
      your age? older? younger?
      your choice or allocated by a school?
      familiar with your mother tongue or not?

- Would you go to him or her or would he or she come to you? At whose convenience?

- Would you travel abroad on a language learning 'package' for a short intensive course?
- What sort of learning environment or milieu would you find conducive?
    Your own home?
    A teacher's living room or study?
    Your office?
    A school classroom?
    A specially designed learning 'studio' comfortable and fully-equipped with all the modern aids and electronics? (video, computer, overhead projector etc)
- What sort of atmosphere or mood would you like your lessons to take place in?
    Cut-and-dried activity with no messing about?
    Intimate and easy-going?
    Teacher or student directed?
    Formal or informal?
    Intensive (time-pressured) with extensive coverage?
    or
    Extensive (spacious) with time to concentrate intensively?
- What sort of relationship would you want with your teacher?
    Professional and cool?
    Personal and warm?
    A bit of both?
- What role would you see your teacher as taking?
    Informer and resource adviser?
    Initiator and director?
    Coach and motivator?
    Trainer and evaluator?
    Authority and explainer?
- What would you expect to **do** in lesson time?
- What would be your real motivation?
  Can you think of any more motives?
- How would your motives differ from those of your actual or prospective students? How do you think they would answer these questions?

Teacher messages

If you have already taught one-to-one you will have many feelings and attitudes, not all of them positive or helpful. It is all too easy for you to send out unhelpful messages, which make your work more difficult. Check yourself, tick those which ring a bell, and add any more you can think of or which you notice yourself giving in the course of a lesson.

"Like me"

"Here we are, thrown together in this room. Well, we'd better get on with it"

"My god, not another workaholic"

"Welcome to your lesson. I'm your teacher"

"I want to sell you my methods"

"If you're not interested in me why should I be in you"

"Now let me seduce you with my charm and personality"

"See how tidy and professional I am"

"You know I'm being extremely patient"

"Right, now it's my turn to resume control of this lesson"

"If only you could see yourself"

"What a relief that's over with"

"Shall we get down to some real work now"

"Look what I've dreamed up for you today"

"You're messing up my lesson plan"

"This is quite a dump isn't it. Well at least we can silently commiserate"

"I've done quite enough for what I'm being paid"

Teacher beliefs

In a similar way, you can too easily worry about **yourself**, your performance, plans, needs and ignore the student. We have aleady discussed that
your main talent should be response-ability . . . Check your needs and
ideas with this list:

- I have only one student so if he or she fails to improve I have failed
- We have only a short time so we had better work fast and hard and try
  to cover as much ground as possible
- My efforts must be commensurate with what the student/company is
  paying
- My efforts need only be commensurate with what I am being paid
- I need to prove to my student that

    I'm in charge

    I'm authoritative

    I'm knowledgeable

    I know his/her language

    I have everything under control and planned

    I'm a professional

- I have to keep things moving all the time
- They all need the same things basically

    good
- I'm a mediocre teacher

    bad

- If I take risks the student will   complain
  think I'm eccentric
  lose trust in me

Tick the beliefs that affect your teaching. Try to think of good reasons for holding beliefs **opposite** to these and to the others listed above.

Things to look for in your interaction with the student

With all **your** beliefs and ideas in mind, here is a check list of how it can affect your interaction in the classroom.

- Are you forcing the pace or lagging behind your student's drive?
- Is your student 'performing' mechanically or with real motivation?
- Are you confident of the 'how' and 'why' of what you are doing and is this confidence shared by your student?
- Are you over-controlling communication or allowing your student to dominate?
- Are you sharing decisions with your student or taking all responsibility on yourself?
- Are you giving your student options, dictating or negotiating the work you do?
- Are you adapting to your student's conversational and working style?
- Is your assessment of your student's motivation accurate or are you guiding yourself and your student by false projections or assumptions?
- Does your student know his or her own motivation clearly and can you help him or her to clarify objectives?
- Do you push on regardless with an activity despite negative signals of boredom, tiredness or dissatisfaction from your student?
- Do you take steps to obtain explicit feedback from your student?
- Do you provide feedback to your student when you realise he or she has a problem?
- Are you on the look-out for topics or activities that the student responds positively to and do you build on these?
- Do you allow work to proceed haphazardly or do you review and re-clarify course objectives whenever necessary?
- Are you aware of your own areas of ignorance, admit and take steps to compensate for these?
- Are there feelings you don't allow yourself in teaching? How much do you restrict or facilitate your own personality and self-expression?
- Do you give your student opportunities to teach you?
- Do you think about what this particular student's manner and personality is teaching you?
- Do you allow yourself to learn from your student?
- Do you give yourself time to recollect your observations and feelings after each working period?
- Do you allow yourself and your student 'off-'days or periods?

- Do you permit yourself breathing space, freedom of movement and sufficient breaks?
- Do you give your student opportunities for work alone without fussing and interfering?

Lesson planning

Lesson planning is fundamentally an art of selection based on a large number of competing considerations. Only in its final stages is it merely a routine or technically thought-out sequencing of activities and stages.

This is particularly true in one-to-one and for the short-intensive course in which curricula and coursebooks give way to a day-by-day re-evaluation and monitoring of a student's strengths and weaknesses, needs and priorities.

Aids, equipment, published material and techniques, topics and curricular points all form part of a vast bank of resources and foci, to which we can add both authentic material and the authentic communication that goes on in one-to-one.

A starting point for lesson planning is the student's personal and professional communicative needs. In the foreground of these lies the language needed to fulfil them. In the background lie the skills, confidence, and manner needed to learn and demonstrate them. An assessment of the needs of an individual must therefore include this centre, background and foreground, and the needs of each.

Considering these the teacher can then select simultaneously the language to be taught or revised, and a communicative activity. The communicative activity is not a means to learning language. It is the other way round. From this point of view it is quite natural and right for the teacher to be asking 'What are we going to *do* in this lesson?' What is basically required is not 'language points' or even 'activities' but a format for communication. This may include language items, or like CLL be an activity in itself, or it may not. In principle a format is any aid, technique or worksheet supplying a frame for the personalisation and professionalisation of language in communication. It is also the natural things that come second to a teacher's mind "I'm going to ask him to use the rods to present his company's organisational structure". Coursebook material and authentic material provide formats also, whether in the form of models for parallel writing, or articles that elicit student input. On the other hand it is extremely rare, even in business or ESP coursebooks to find *anything* that, in itself is 'tailor-made' for a given individual, rather than a given *category* of individuals.

Having chosen a format for communication, as well as a subject and task, and determined the language that is critical for these, the next important consideration is one of mode (see page 56). The mode of classroom teaching can never be quite the same as the mode of one-to-one. The contrast is best summed up by the two words 'elicitation' and 'facilitation'. Elicitation is a manipulative activity appropriate, if at all, only in the classroom. One can elicit from students, but one should facilitate a student. The difference may appear to be a fine one, and it is ... a razor's edge. Elicitation is part of the game of teacher one-upmanship that has so many variations. Facilitation can also express itself in many modes, but places the teacher firmly in a position that is one-down, student-led, not servile but definitely seeking to serve rather than deliver and impose. Teacher demonstration and student presentation are two modes each of which can be imposed or carried out facilitatively. The question of mode recognises the importance of the authentic communication of student and teacher for the teaching of anything. The modes and tenor of communication that form part of the lesson plan are there to oil the wheels of natural communication, replenish its sources, or simply provide breathing spaces. To prevent the lesson becoming dry and void of meaning. To keep student and teacher really in contact with each other. You may like to find your own names for the different modes in which any given activity or theme can be introduced and handled.

Just as there is more to communication than language, more to a format than an activity (space for student input), and more to the how than to the what (mode), so too there is more to the '4 skills' than meets the eye, or the ear. Coursebooks are basically a combination of formats and auditing steps. There is more variation to auditing than the words 'reading', 'writing', 'speaking' and 'listening' imply. The teacher cannot rely on the auditing procedures in a coursebook unit being the ones that really train the student in the skills he or she needs most improvement in. The teacher must audit the coursebooks, and in effect create a personal one for each student by the end of his or her course. The checklist of auditing procedures included in this book is there as a reminder of what sort of things one can add to the exercises and activities that coursebook units contain, and ways one can independently devise procedures and routes for processing its material. They also suggest ways of utilising authentic material, not only company or specialised literature but 'real' books and cassettes, journals and videos of all sorts, especially business books and business programmes recorded by video.

If we are in the business of language teaching the product of lessons is another consideration. By product I mean both tangible and intangible end-results. Tangible take-away products include sets of cards, worksheets, articles, transcripts and tapes. The intangible products return us to the question of student needs, the aim of a lesson or course. What is necessary is to be able to visualise the product of an activity in terms of what one knows about him or her, as well as to provide a product in tangible form that gives the student as such a *hold* on the returns that the lesson has aimed for. At the end of the course it would be a mark of consideration to provide the student with a bound collation of worksheets, copies and material constituting a retrospective coursebook that can be reviewed and reworked. The student has his or her own completed worksheets but these cannot be reworked and nor is the other material likely to be seriously reviewed in its disorganised loose-leaf form unless the student is encouraged to do so, by the care and suggestion implied by collation and binding of an extra set.

Last but not least in the considerations that play a vital role in lesson planning are the teacher's needs. Making the multiple choices necessary for lesson planning and realisation requires basically a trust in one's own impulses and intuitions. Feeling can decide where logic alone would be overloaded with reasons for and against. Learning to decide one's teaching spontaneously is like learning to speak a foreign language spontaneously. There is no harm in going for what *you* find satisfying, interesting, meaningful rather than sacrificing this to what you *think* the student will. Again it is a question here of the authenticity with which you present material and engage with the student in lesson activities. Communication is a two-sided affair. Without your full involvement the

NEVER MIND THE STUDENT, WHAT ABOUT **ME** ?

student is not going to be motivated either. Because your teaching, however well-intentioned, will not communicate.

Different formats, modes, and procedures work differently with different students. Some of the ideas mentioned in this book may be new to you and new to your student. Do not expect the same result or the same reception from every student and you won't be disappointed. If you are trying out an idea for the first time, decide in advance the attitude and 'modes' you will adopt, and maintain this attitude as you do the activity. If you are clear about the manner and mood in which you wish the activity to proceed you will give yourself and your student the psychological support to carry it through. If, despite this you do not meet with success you will at least know this is not due to your own ambivalence, and can try the activity again with a different student, in a different mode, or with a different attitude.

Teacher aims

No lesson is complete unless it includes not just a true aim for the student but also an aim for the teacher, for you. The basic question is: *What difference do I want to make to my teaching this morning, today, this week, with this student?* Satisfying teacher aims brings teacher satisfaction and a satisfied teacher makes for a satisfied student. There are many examples of teacher aims, from simply trying out new materials and aids, to trying out new beliefs. Here are some examples to whet your appetite.

- Trying out a new seating position.
- Taking off my teacher mask for a time.
- Using music.
- Designing an activity that needs no correction.
- Teaching in silence.
- Standing up and moving around when my body feels restless.
- Exploring the role of eye-contact in speech.

- Really tuning in to my student and listening to what he or she says at the start of the lesson.
- Noticing which me I leave behind or suppress when the student arrives or when I enter my school.
- Observing my gestures/language in the course of a lesson.
- Observing my student's gestures and habits.
- Teaching the student a non-linguistic skill.
- Giving the student a choice.
- Teaching for a while without TEFL material.
- Teaching the way I imagine another teacher teaches.
- Filling in an important piece of missing information about my student.
- Spending 10 minutes after the lesson recording subtle observations that occurred to me during it.
- Getting feedback from my student.
- Tracing my mood and energy in the course of a lesson.
- Improving my transitions from one activity to another.

Choose 3 teacher aims that you wish to realise and make notes on how you will go about this.

Teaching modes

The concept of mode was introduced earlier. It affects both teacher and student, and the interaction between them. Here is a selection of modes, each appropriate to different circumstances and for different people. Have you tried them all? Could you introduce more variety into **your** teaching?

The conversational mode

Here the teacher adopts a conversational attitude and tone with all that this implies. Communication is relaxed, low-key and natural, with the teacher adopting his or her own natural speech manner. Language may still be graded but pronunciation is natural. The teacher may sit next to rather than opposite the student, working together. The conversational mode is not just 'for conversation', but is a mode of teaching with the minimum of artificiality and role division: always a positive aim to strive for.

The instructional mode
Conversational teaching will not be appropriate at all times and for all purposes. Teaching the phonemic chart, for example, or working with beginners. There comes a point at which the downgrading of language restricts or altogether rules out the conversational mode, except for a few "politeness" phrases. The instructional mode on the other hand, is not restricted in relevance to low-level students. Many executives are not only used to but expect an instructional mode. These expectations may be either a result of their school experience or alternatively reflect the dominant mode of management training which they have experienced.

The caretaker mode
This means not only grading one's language as a teacher but also slowing down one's speech, adding extra emphasis to words, intonation and articulation. Caretaker speech has its real dangers: particularly where the emphasis of speech reflects a teaching point but runs counter to natural stress and intonation. The result is that one error replaces another. The student 'takes the point' but in the process mimics the teacher's unnatural word- or sentence-stress. There is nothing to be said against slowing down speech however. Slowed-down speech can be of great value to the student in revealing the true, natural contours of pitch and phonemic constitution of an utterance. Its use should be deliberate and extreme, so the student knows what is normal and what is not.

The lets-have-fun-together mode
Appropriate to language games in particular it may also reflect a general attitude to teaching which is that it should be fun, exciting, energetic, active, pleasurable. How much this mode comes into our teaching is very much a personal question. If it reflects *you* ie your general experience of life, fine. But one man's 'fun' may be another's 'boredom', and this applies to both teacher and student. Knowing what you find pleasure in is important. Artificial 'joie-de-vivre' is deadly.

The serious-professional-business mode
This can be equally misplaced or over-extended. Your students may be serious about learning, and may be professional businessmen. But they are also individuals with their own personality and values. There is no point trying to impress them with your own business-like approach or impersonality. The central point is to adapt to the student's **personality** not his or her 'position' or 'role'.

The dramatic mode
An alternative to the caretaker mode, this works by adding dramatic rather than pedagogic emphasis and gesture to speech. Learning to put meaning, gesture and emotion—movement—into speech is a valuable art, serving real-life situations (public speaking, for example) as well as teaching. Once again however, it should be used sparingly or within definite and clear boundaries. The better actor you are, the more likely you are to over-awe your student with too much of the dramatic mode.

The teacher

The silent mode

The informal mode

The regimental mode

· · · · · · · · · · · · · · · · · · · ·

How many more modes can you think of? Make a point of thinking in terms of mode when you plan lessons and as you get to know your student.

Your basic attitude—one-upmanship?

One common criticism of 'communicative' teaching is that it lacks visibility: students just can't see 'the method' in the same way as they could perhaps in school, with audio-visual or grammar translation lessons. The emphasis on doing things with language rather than talking about it becomes dangerous however, as soon as it is considered as a license to *manipulate* students into producing language without *explanation* of any whats, whys or wherefores. Of course any sort of explaining is difficult at beginner or elementary levels but then at this stage of the game less is necessary, for the purpose of a given language activity or teacher 'trick' is usually transparent and its value self-evident. This is not always the case, and certainly not at higher levels and with students who may, through no fault of their own, and no lack of intelligence whatsoever, nevertheless lack the support of any guiding thread such as the idea of language 'functions' and 'notions'.

We need not consider it beneath our own or our students dignity to explain things that we have learnt to understand as obvious. For example that the prime value of a language course is not just learning to make fewer and fewer mistakes but rather using more of the language and using it in a more economical and effective way. A good comparison here is the computer. Making good use of a computer does not mean becoming a faultless typist, able to key-in data without a slip. The point is to know the machine and know its potentials. To be able to call upon language potentials in a way that suits one's own particular language needs is the object of the student. The software or programming instructions that the teacher provides must also have this object in mind, for any language contains unlimited potential from which the teacher must be able to extract only that which is most relevant and useful. Software exercises the computer in highly specific ways which vary enormously according to the purpose it serves. There is no such thing as 'General Software', and in this sense there is no such thing as 'General English', for even the most elementary programming instructions ('grammar') must be applied in specific contexts.

Above all the student needs to feel a sense of achievement in learning to manipulate the language. For the teacher this comes more or less naturally. The teacher is therefore automatically 'one-up', an authority or expert. Or is (s)he? The student may indeed feel so, tempting the teacher to employ all sorts of conventional 'tricks' which make the student, and not the language, an object of manipulation. For example, so-called 'elicitation' techniques which demand that the student in some way guess the language which the teacher wants the student to produce. As a way of presenting new language, these are, in my opinion to be avoided or at least handled in such a way as to avoid oneupmanship. The idea of exposing the student's lack of a certain bit of language in order then to come to the rescue by generously handing it over is questionable in itself, but especially so in the one-to-one relationship where the one-up status of the teacher is not something to be exacerbated by any sort of guessing game . . . unless this be reversible and can place the teacher in the position of being one-down!

This 'interrogative' or 'elicitative' style of teaching may be suitable for groups, where sheer weight of numbers balances the power of the teacher. In one-to-one it all too easily becomes interrogation, a strain on both teacher and student. The sort of questioning that rides on a 'one-up' position for the teacher needs to be thoughtfully transformed into questioning and relating from a position of equality. And this means recognising also the *one-down* position of the teacher.

In this process you must be prepared to share more of your own individual world than is customary in teaching. Every type of *personalisation* of language is, of course, wonderfully suited to one-to-one. Your student's biography, current life with its future possibilities, and probabilities, hopes, intentions and regrets provides ample material for practising all the tenses and notions of English. It is your role, however, to take the lead in this sharing. It will be a teacher-student exchange, not a student-student one . . . and you may be surprised what your student can teach you! This is important also for properly assessing motivation. In group teaching it may be sufficient to distinguish the highly motivated from the less well or poorly motivated student. In one-to-one such quantitative assessment of degrees of motivation proves quite inadequate. A student may be strongly committed to his or her career and a self-confessed 'workaholic' and yet in no way identify with that work. Whilst acknowledging a need for English in business or professional contexts, (s)he may be more interested in life, travel, and learning about other countries, peoples, and lifestyles.

It is important to know whether the student has volunteered for this course or been 'sent'; whether (s)he has paid personally, or is covered by the company. Remember also that (s)he may be taking time off from holidays, sacrificing anything up to his or her entire holiday entitlement to come and work hard at English. Alternatively, or additionally, (s)he may come bringing along personal or professional needs, problems or worries of which you know little or nothing.

It may be that your student feels very much 'one-down', anxious and insecure to an almost neurotic degree, or insistent on being always one-up, as a compensation for such insecurities. I have had students who have not merely requested but demanded that our whole time be spent working through a grammar textbook. Others who wish only to chat. Most people in one-to-one will recognise 'types'. Those who fall in between the extremes however challenge us to a different type of sensitivity. Can the student pace himself/herself? Does (s)he know when (s)he's had enough of something? How aware is (s)he of physical and mental needs: for rest, for diversion, for physical activity or refreshment?

EXCUSE ME... SORRY... I MUST GO
ANOTHER PLACE... BUT I
AM COMING BACK!

Is (s)he self-regulating, or must you take care that (s)he either does not overdo it or 'gets down to it' with a little more guided concentration? Is (s)he an absorber, an 'acquirer', or a 'learner', studious or vivacious or both?

For in one-to-one all the debates in applied linguistics and language teaching about learning and acquisition, accuracy and fluency, orthodox versus fringe approaches, boil down to one thing: one individual, and another—the individual teacher. What is food for one student may be poison for the other. In one-to-one we have the chance to adapt and find the right balance of apparently opposite approaches to suit each student and to maintain an overall position that is neither one-up nor one-down, but *one-to-one*.

As a general rule we should be aware of the role that any given exercise or activity puts us in and use our most powerful variable—the amount of *correction* we give, to minimise the one-up/one-down effect. The student may desire constant correction, but for the wrong reasons. Sensitivity and desire for correction are one thing. So also is what the student does with it. With some it makes all the difference; with others none. So again, it is *your* sensitivity to the individual that counts rather than abstract principles.

Even so, we cannot fail to be aware how much greater opportunity for correction the one-to-one situation provides, and bring the appropriate caution to it. Naturally it is not what we correct or even how much that is crucial but the way in which we do it. This is where we really need our adult selves as an ally, to set a tone of quiet, respectful and helpful correction that contributes to, rather than blocks and interrupts, the flow of communication, interaction and dialogue.·

Just as the student often has difficulty in 'finding the word'; in calling upon or pin-pointing the language he needs, so will you, the teacher need time to really get a clear enough picture of the student's world, language needs and language difficulties, and, particularly, *what turns this individual on,* his or her 'style'. You will need to experiment with a variety of approaches before anything like a working routine is established. To do so involves risk, the risk of failing, the risk of being one-down. But it offers also the possibility of genuinely negotiating the working day from a position of equality and shared responsibility: offering the student options for example, and asking for feedback and self-assessment. In a very real sense, every student in one-to-one is your teacher. By the end of the course, if it has been successful, you will end up having learnt many new and valuable things: your repertoire of techniques and approaches will have increased as will your range of what might be called teacher *personae*. Your style will be enriched, more fluid and adaptable. You will have got the message, overcome the challenge and learnt the lessons that arose from having observed and appreciated the uniqueness of another individual; and having had to respond to that uniqueness every minute of the day.

Avoid Oneupmanship

- Share your reasons and your understanding: your experience.

- Don't let your student have to guess what you want him or her to say or do. Avoid 'elicitation' as a means of *presenting* new language. TEACH BEFORE YOU TEST!

- Manipulate the material not the student!

- Use analogies to offer tips and explanations (eg the computer).

- Make sure that all games you use are reversible. For example '20 Questions'. Let the student think of a mystery object/job/person *first*. This way (s)he is 'one up' and you have a chance to demonstrate the type of questions (s)he can later ask.

- Personalise the Notions of English. And be the first to do so. Do not ask the student to use language to describe aspects of his or her life without doing so first yourself.

- Remember that at the start of the course you are 'one down'! Respect and learn about . . . learn from . . . your student's existential world. Let each student teach you the approach that (s)he needs.

- Allow the working day to be *self-regulating* and not controlled by any idea, plan or person. Know what you want to achieve or do, and let the time for it arise spontaneously and naturally. Trust that this will happen rather than "forcing the pace".

- Follow, don't fight, your impulses, moods and energy level.

- Be selective in correction. Remember that it's 'not what you do but the way that you do it'.

- Engage in activities from a position of contact with the student. If this contact is lost so will the activity. Activities should not be a substitute for, but an expression of, contact.

- Offer options in deciding activities.

- Provide activities which give a sense of real achievement or which allow the student to feel 'one-up'.

- Take risks. Experiment. You will need to find out what works for this individual.

- Don't try and be a model or perfect teacher. Perfectionism is the *worst* model to present to your student.

- Teach the student to learn without a teacher. For example try letting the student 'take the wheel' with a textbook unit.

The teacher

Your needs

In concluding this chapter, however, it is important to return to **your** needs. Teachers (you!) are also people, and the interchange of the one-to-one classroom will die if **either** of the participants fails to behave as a full person. While you may be paid to take part unequally in the interchange, so that the student's linguistic and other needs take first place, you are not paid to remain totally frustrated, inhibited and excluded. You cannot **give** to the student unless you too are drawing satisfaction, and even pleasure from the interchange. Here is a brief check list of your own needs which may clarify your thinking in times of frustration:

- Is this interesting?
- Who can **I** talk to?
- What's the challenge?
- Where shall I sit?
- What are **my** aids for this lesson?
- What material to make it work
  for **both** of us?
- What excites or interests **me**
  about tomorrow's encounter?

In the end, one-to-one only works for **either** participant if it is truly a learning exchange, so that there is no need to feel guilty about thinking about, and taking into real consideration, **your** needs as well as those of your "client".

4. Preparations before the course begins

Many one-to-one students are professionals, and reasonably expect a similarly professional attitude to their course. This means careful thought about:
  —pre-course information for the teacher
  —equipment
  —the physical environment

Both teacher and student are likely to be more relaxed, and the early part of the course more productive, if adequate preparations have been made. This means information about the student being available to the teacher (not just the school) in advance; adequate, but not restrictive, consideration of language materials before the student arrives and adequate practical preparation of the room.

One-to-one teaching can be intensive and psychologically cramped. Every effort must be made to minimise this. Preparing the room and seating, and choosing effective equipment, which is also **small**, can help to create a feeling of spaciousness which is most likely to be conducive to effective and enjoyable study.

Finally, teachers need to prepare *themselves* by reflecting on the way their attitudes and behaviour can contribute to, or inhibit, the success of any course.

Preparations

Things you can obtain on or before Day 1

- prospectuses and brochures

- promotional material

- in-house journals

- trade-journals

- product descriptions

- product samples

- technical manuals

- examples of correspondence

- taped telephone calls

- minutes of meetings

- reports and plans:
    profit and loss
    balance sheets
    projections
    marketing plans

- details of local subsidiaries, parent or sister companies

- personal material:
    cv
    photographs
    maps/guides to student's home region

If a student is given a questionnaire before joining a one-to-one course it is extremely important that the questionnaire is filled in by the individual student, and not by a training manager who can give only generalised answers.

It is also worth considering carefully the design of such questionnaires. There is a temptation to put straightforward factual information first, but there is something to be said for putting more interesting questions first in order to catch the student's attention and encourage them to see the importance and usefulness of the questionnaire.

Using the pre-course material

Students taking one-to-one for business or special purposes can be sent a list such as this and asked to indicate which of the items they can and will provide and when. The use of such material in lessons may prove entirely unnecessary or unwelcome for the student depending on his or her real goals and motivation. On the other hand there will be cases when it makes all the difference, so it is essential to be prepared. In such cases the student often recognises the importance of bringing materials along, but this cannot be relied upon.

Alternatively the really important information that a student may supply about his or her language needs may be of a confidential nature and shared orally with the teacher in the course of their interaction. An example is 'inside' information about company plans or negotiations which should not become the common knowledge of competitors. Alternatively the material passed on may be quite public, perhaps promotional, and yet be well-suited to work within lessons.

In examining such materials to assess their usefulness for the student there are three aspects to take into account: the format, the content, and the language.

The format may be anything from a set of numbered diagrams of machine parts to a sample of a new brand of paper handkerchief.

The content may be technical or financial, confidential or promotional, comprehensible or abstruse.

The language may or may not reflect the student's communicative needs. It may be L1 or L2.

For the teacher the most important thing is to distinguish the student's professional language from his or her communicative needs. Teaching a student the language he or she needs and teaching a student to communicate in L2 are not the same thing. How closely or distantly related they are will vary in each case and depend on the communicative *tasks* facing the student. At one extreme we might have a student who in fact is required to write exactly the sort of specialised material supplied in advance to the teacher or school. At the other extreme there are those students whose 'professional purposes' turn out in fact to be entirely secondary to other motivations and who are interested principally in social English or in taking a holiday. In between we find students who may be more or less familiar with their own specialised languages, or whose use of this language is entirely conditioned by specific positions, roles and situations.

It could be said that the ideal teacher for one-to-one is not only linguistically aware and trained to teach but also bilingual and a specialist in the student's own field. This would be an ideal combination of talents, but at its heart lies precisely the ability to correctly gauge communicative needs, and to apply and teach the *skills* required by students to achieve this combination *themselves*. These *are* precisely those skills which the teacher *is* competent to teach.

Things you can do before day 1

- Find out your student's name, age and suposed level
- Find out your student's job and nationality
- Obtain a copy of his or her application/registration form
- Obtain any professional material that your student can or has supplied
- Obtain any test material completed by your student
- Conduct a prior interview if possible
- Speak to anyone who knows or has spoken to the student if possible
- Obtain any file that may exist on the student, or on his or her company, or speciality
- Audit the above information—see p. 22
- Audit the student's L1 if this is unfamilair to you
- Audit any coursebook or other material that may be relevant to this student's needs

In this context auditing means examining with particular emphasis on the implications for language *form*. What kind of lexis is likely to be appropriate for the student? What kind of *specific* situation is (s)he likely to face? What kind of interference mistakes are likely, bearing in mind the student's L1?

It is never possible to predict in advance what an individual one-to-one student will need; as we have already said the chief skill is the teacher's response-ability. At the same time, part of the teacher's general responsibility is to examine all materials which are available in advance critically from a language point of view, in order to ensure maximum possible advance preparation for the student's needs.

- Gather authentic material that may be useful (eg if you are teaching an optician, visit an opticians)
- Use public libraries for specialised reference sources
- Check the available language teaching literature for special purpose texts
- Ensure the availability of any dictionaries, general or specialised, mono- and bi-lingual that may be required
- Ensure the availability of any equipment that you may wish to use
- Collate, design, copy or reformat material you may require on day 1
- Check the room you will be using for ventilation, adequate seating and desk space, room for equipment, electrical sockets, lighting and heating, noise etc.
- Obtain or put in requests for additional items of furniture, decor, equipment, or conveniences
- Decide on a seating arrangement

- Make all copies in good time
- Make necessary enquiries regarding any visits you could arrange for your student

Things to consider in auditing coursebook material in advance

- Does your use of the material contribute to an overall course objective?
- Will it be seen to do so, or can its usefulness be explained?
- Can the units be gone through systematically and in sequence?
- If there are too many units for a course which are of most relevance to the student?
- Is the language presented within a unit relevant to this student's needs?
- Is the language contained within the unit's texts or dialogues relevant?
- Is the topic relevant?
- Are the exercises and activities appropriate: do they practise the relevant skills?
- Can the activities be adapted to one-to-one work?
- Does the material interest you?
- Are the activities interesting?
- Will they stimulate/interest/motivate your student?
- Does the material provide space for student input: can it stimulate discussion or provide a model for parallel writing or language transfer?
- Are you sufficiently familiar with it?
- Has familiarity already bred contempt?
- Does it suggest useful preparatory or follow-up work?
- Does it *present* language or allow the student to *discover* language?
- Can you anticipate the difficulties your student might encounter with it?
- Does it include necessary speechwork and pronunciation exercises?
- Does it provide opportunities for encouraging the student to practise useful auditing skills?
- Is the format helpful?
- Can you photocopy and reformat the material in accordance with your own ideas and instructions for exploitation?
- Have you time to audit or re-format it thoroughly?

Useful Equipment

- **Pens.** These should include at least two highlighter pens in different colours which the student can use to mark words and phrases. For marking features of pronunciation or writing in several colours an extremely useful item, for teacher and student, is a 4-colour ballpoint, such as the very reliable and cheap version manufactured by BIC.

- **A Walkman cassette-recorder.** If possible with radio. A basic Walkman recorder is an invaluable and inexpensive piece of equipment. The student can easily take it in hand for transcription work or self-recording, as well as using it for interviews, on visits, and for aural and oral homework. Its portability encourages casual use and out-of-class listening, as well as easy transfer from person to person.

- **Radio.** Radio-recorders are a lot more expensive than a basic Walkman, but some facility for recording news and other items is essential. Again, the smaller size of the Walkman allows the student to take it home and record things, as well as permitting out-of-class listening. Headphones should be provided for use both in and out of class.

- **Twin-cassette recorders,** of the larger type, usually include a radio. Schools should have at least one of these available for the copying facility and/or radio-recording. High-speed tape-to-tape recording is advisable to save time.

- **Whiteboard and coloured dry-wipe marker pens.** Small and inexpensive versions of these are available from art shops and office suppliers if you are working at home. Essential for 'get up and write it' activity, not only for the teacher but for the student who can do draft work on the board which is easily corrected before transferring to paper.

- **Telephone.** It would be a great boon if schools offering one-to-one tuition to executives would have available at least one telephone for lesson use (ie not a payphone and not the school's office phone). Business people are used to having their own phones and these provide a great incentive to actually doing telephone work. Pretend telephoning is no substitute for the real thing, which offers opportunities for authentic recording of calls, recorded messages and numerous service lines ranging from weather forecasts to financial hotlines and the BBC news itself.

- **Telephone pick-up.** Can be used in class or by the teacher for recording authentic telephone conversations, eg arrangements for visits made before student arrives, enquiry calls, talks with friends etc. A cordless phone is the ideal modern solution. This can be shared between office and teaching staff, and taken from room to room according to need.

- **Cuisenaire rods.** These are almost as basic as pens and paper or a cassette recorder. They are coloured wooden rods, originally designed for the teaching of mathematics. Some teachers may be familiar with them in language teaching where they are used in the Silent Way. Conjurers distinguish between stage illusions and 'close-up' magic involving the manipulation of small objects. The rods come in the latter category, and are therefore particularly suited for use in one-to-one work. They are a tangible, and highly adaptable format for student presentation. They may be used to represent objects, company structure, etc. for language features such as phonemes, morphemes, word order etc. Their uses are discussed on page 120.

  The rods are available from educational suppliers, or by post from the Cuisenaire Company Ltd., 11 Crown Street, Reading, RG1 2TQ.

- **Typewriter.** Useful and important not only for preparing teaching materials but especially for producing readable and professional 'copy' of student writing. Can be used for taking dictation from the student in lesson time (see *Things you can do with dictation*). A light portable model is obviously recommendable, as are the so-called 'Graphwriters', which will draw graphs from figures keyed in by either student or teacher as part of a business listening or speaking exercise. Graphwriters form part of the Brother, Canon, and Silver Reed ranges of portables, and are amongst the cheapest. The Brother model offers an extra large font which provides excellent copy for presentations which are to be read aloud.

In addition to the items listed the provision of an in-tray (or 'in' and 'out' trays) is also recommended. Materials prepared or copied in advance for the student can be placed in the in-tray. For executive students in particular this reproduces a familiar workstyle, offers the opportunity for choice of work and at least a partial overview of what the course holds in store. Teachers can write letters to their students in a variety of formats from postcard to formal report and for a variety of purposes including giving feedback to students or obtaining it from them. Completed worksheets, replies to letters, and 'processed' materials can be passed to the out-tray for checking, collating, and perhaps typing.

The list may seem a long one but in fact its rationale, like that of the in-tray, is to reduce desk clutter and avoid mountains of heavy equipment and coursebooks, each of which may be 90 percent redundant to a particular student's needs or contain far too many units for a short course. The desk space between teacher and student should have space. *One* aid or piece of equipment and/or an in-tray should be sufficient for any given activity. Everything else should be placed elsewhere, though conveniently in reach.

Rooms for one-to-one should therefore include some storage or shelf space, as well as plants and pictures to create an attractive focus or rest for the eye. Everything, in other words that might be expected in a reasonably comfortable office, however spartan or empty in other respects. Sitting at a desk with your student is the principal hallmark of one-to-one teaching. It is worthwhile considering and finding out just what sort of work-space your students themselves are used to, especially those with business or professional careers. Chairs as such are an important 'ergonomic' consideration for you as well as your student. So-called 'back chairs' would be ideal for avoiding postural strain over long periods, but at the very least one wants desk chairs with arms and comfortable seats.

Creating space for learning

It is easy for the one-to-one situation to become claustrophobic. This may result both from such physical considerations as a tiny cluttered room, or from the psychology of being "cooped up" with one other person for hours on end. This claustrophobia can easily inhibit both teacher and student, and render lessons less pleasurable and less effective. As far as possible, the teacher should try to counteract the claustrophobia with a deliberate attempt to create space for learning.

The "space" which is created, like the claustrophobia, can be both physical and psychological. The reader is invited to consider what *practical* meaning each of the following types of "space" could have in the context of one-to-one teaching. Pause for a moment, and on a large (spacious?) piece of blank paper make your own notes on possible ways of creating space under the following headings:

- space for movement
- sensory space
- student-learning space
- space for listening
- space for student input

- desk space
- imaginative space
- mental and emotional space
- space for recollection
- communicative space

Can you think of other ways in which space can be created, and an enabling rather than inhibiting atmosphere be encouraged? My own suggestions are summarized on pages 74 and 75.

Intolerable, and this for smokers as well as non-smokers, are rooms with inadequate ventilation, windows that cannot be opened or which serve as a barrier against deafening traffic sounds and fumes. I say this because almost every school I have worked in has had this problem, and it really is a problem that needs dealing with. The brain requires oxygen, and stale air, smoke-filled or not, is a hindrance to energy and work. The use of ionisers for cleaning and freshening the air would go some way to improving the situation, if windows really cannot be unsealed.

There are teachers who work at home in their living rooms and those who work in school or company rooms. The ideal 'language studio' contains elements and permits something of the feeling of all three. With larger rooms a division into areas is possible: a storage area, space for standing, role play and speech work, a 'living room' area with low reclining chairs and coffee table, a video corner and/or computer workstation, perhaps a self-access area with books and tapes. If you do work at home you can think along these lines. But even if you can't, it helps to *visualise* an ideal of this sort, for by doing so we can cultivate the sort of *feeling* and atmosphere which we wish to experience and create in our teaching.

Space, relaxation, and an effective working environment have to do with more than physical surroundings. There are more personal elements to the teacher's preparation as well.

Manner, modes, moves

As in every teaching situation the personality and attitudes of the teacher find expression in the manner of his or her teaching. This may be serious or light-hearted, casual or strict, informal or formal, withdrawn or outgoing, speedy or slow, awkward or graceful, anxious or calm, calm or energetic, relaxed or intense, active or receptive, spontaneous or controlled. Manner is also influenced by internal factors such as mood and by the physical, social and psychological environment of the room, school, institution, town or country. This is what I call the 'milieu'. A teacher's gestures and manner carry certain messages, and are a basic part of the communication of teacher and student. The milieu itself carries its own messages and connotations. It may be warm or cool, domestic or professional, drab or colourful, spartan or comfortable, friendly or formal.

The student's manner may be a response to the milieu, or to the manner of the teacher, or a question of mood or motivation. It cannot be expected that the student is at all used to sitting in a room with a teacher for several hours. Finding the right manner to respond to, relax, move and motivate a particular student may require trial and error as well as experimentation with different methods of work. It helps to visualise the student in his or her ordinary working environment and get a picture of what would constitute an ordinary working day in the life of this person. Matching our manner, methods and workstyle with that of the student always means bearing in mind cultural differences as well. Verbal stereotypes aside, there *are* differences between French, Spanish, German, and Japanese students. To have a sense of where this person is 'coming from' is vital, in all senses and on all levels.

Whereas the teacher's manner is a one-sided thing, what I call the *mode* of teaching is something that involves the student too. Though the teacher may use changes in manner to initiate changes in working mode it is the latter that signal the end of one phase of a lesson and the start of another.

Changes in mode go along with changes in the lesson activity, with transitions from doing one thing to doing another. But they are not the same thing. A drill, for example, is an activity which can be carried out in any number of different manners. It is this combination of a new activity with a new manner, a new 'what' with a new 'how', which defines mode.

It makes a difference whether we pass from a 'serious' reading exercise to a 'light-hearted drill' or from a 'light-hearted' bit of reading to a 'serious' drill. We have not fully prepared for a lesson or cannot handle transitions within lessons effectively unless we anticipate or create changes in manner to match the deployment of new methods or the introduction of new activities.

Modes are manners of working together with a student in one-to-one

They range from a 'solo' mode in which we leave the student alone to get on with it, to informal, casual or conversational modes, through to 'serious professional collaboration'. Labelling modes is more difficult than labelling manner and mood, for we are talking about a type of interaction rather than either one of the persons interacting. A 'working together' mode, rather than a 'solo' or 'teacher-instructing-student' mode may or may not be easy to establish; similarly a 'playing-games' mode. It all depends on the student as well as the teacher. And that is the essential point. Variety and correct choice of mode is our means of maintaining and developing student *involvement* in the lesson.

Leaving-the-student-to-get-on with it, for example, is just as much a way of working together and of ensuring student involvement in the work as any other mode.

Changes in lesson mode may often be marked by actual movements, and can be consciously signalled and initiated by these. This is the most practical way of understanding mode and extending variety of mode. The moves a teacher makes can be divided as follows:

Head movements: nodding, raising, lowering

Trunk movements: leaning forward and back in a chair

Chair movements: altering the angle to the student

Positional movements: changing seats or seating arrangements by going from desk to armchairs, switching seats

Whole-body movements: getting up, sitting down, moving around

Postural changes: involving arms and legs

Gestures: with arms, hands, fingers.

The exact words we use to describe these divisions are not important. The manner in which we carry them out, the message they bear to the student and their impact on teaching *mode* is. Awareness is important.

Moves reflect manner and establish modes. There is no point in trying to establish a more relaxed mode of working with a student if your manner and moves do not correspond to this. On the other hand we can apply the principle: 'create the effect and the cause will follow'. Instead of moving into armchairs because you both feel relaxed, move into them in a relaxed way . . . create the effect . . . and a more relaxed mode will follow.

The teacher may not have to take the initiative in moving: some students like to get up often and 'patrol' the room. But the teacher must respond to the student's moves in a way that is conducive to their joint work, whether this means staying put or mirroring the student. Usually, however it is the student who unconsciously mirrors the physical movements of the teacher at every turn, or who awaits signals that free movement or initiating positional changes are permissible.

It is within this context of the inner bearing of the teacher and how this is reflected in gesture, posture and positional changes that the question of seating must be seen. Starting positions for one-to-one revolve either around a pair of armchairs or a table and chairs . . . preferably both. As far as the table is concerned there are four positions to choose from:

1. facing the student directly on opposite sides
2. facing the student diagonally on opposite sides
3. sitting at right angles to the student
4. sitting next to the student

Different teachers have their favourite or customary positions. The important thing is knowing why, how and when to change: to move as well as to be clear about the starting position you intend to adopt. If one had to give labels to the mood and modes corresponding to these positions I would suggest the following:

1. Role polarisation
2. Moderated role polarisation
3. Tension reducing
4. Collaborative or supportive intimacy

The spectrum ranges from sharp polarisation to intimacy. Position 4 could be appropriate in working supportively with beginners or collaboratively with advanced students.

Position 3 is flexible in terms of the role division or modes of working that it can support, but if the table is rectangular may be counter-productive because of the physical restriction of movement or space for either teacher or student.

Position 1 means sitting face to face with the student. I have called this the role polarisation because it can encourage this and because other positions can be used to soften this polarisation. With an insufficiently broad table it is unavoidable. With a large enough table, Position 2 is probably preferable.

Though many teachers start off in 1, 3 is a favourite position for reducing tension by avoidance of face-to-face contact. Sitting in angled armchairs is an alternative for this purpose, possibly with a small table in between for placing books or papers.

I imagine that position 4 would be considered bold, and that it is the least tried or used position. Again, a large enough table is a pre-requisite, but given this it lends itself to moves designed to reduce role polarisation and enhance the message that 'we're in this together'.

Summary

Suggestions for creating space for learning:

- Make sure your table/desk top does not take away space for 'get up and do it' activities. Move it near a window if possible.

- Decide if you will sit opposite or at right angles to your student. Some students prefer the latter, and this may be necessary if you are sharing books or studying materials.

- If the room is bare or drab bring something to liven it up: posters, pictures and plants. Wall charts (home-made or commercial) can also be very useful.

- If you have a larger space available or are working in a living room plan your use of space accordingly: make use of armchairs to create a more relaxed atmosphere or for passive listening.

- Plan for breaks at more or less regular intervals: not only the twice daily coffee break, but more frequent and briefer pauses for a quick 'get up and stretch' routine.

- Make sure there is a white/blackboard available. If there is not, make a fuss about it. This is *essential* equipment not only for clear presentation but to create a sense of space by allowing both teacher and student to 'get up and write' and by providing a *focus* in space.

- Occasionally swop seats or alter seating positions (for example during a writing exercise or when the student is using the board). As well as providing a change this can have symbolic value (student as teacher!)

- Adopt the attitude right at the start that *you can't do everything* in a short course. You'll feel better as a result and it will allow you to really *give time* to your student. More real progress will be achieved this way.

- Make full use of silence, gesture and pausing in your own speech so that your own language penetrates. There need be nothing inauthentic in a way of speaking that is considered, graceful and poignant or dramatic.

- Make frequent use of writing activities for your student's own benefit. Writing is an excellent form of creative silence, of giving time for thought.

- Use variety to create a constant balance between absorption in the work (reverie), concentration on the work (effort), and recovery from the work (moving on to other things).

- Use your intuition and your own mood and energy level to guide your pacing and choice of activities. If you are bored or strained, the chances are your student will be too.

- Do not feel that you need to fill every minute. Allow spaces in time. Feel free to 'get up and move around' and your students will allow themselves to relax too.

Here is an alternative summary, looking at different kinds of 'Space'.

Desk space	Keeping desk or table free of clutter and awesome textbooks. Adopting a 'minimalist' strategy, using minimal aids and equipment, for example the Walkman recorder.
Space for movement	Encouraging and allowing yourself and the student freedom of movement. Not being glued to a chair or to any one position. Space for movement is space for relaxation.
Sensory space	Not putting up with spartan or drab cells. Respecting needs for sensory stimuli and providing a positive suggestive environment for learning.
Communicative space	Responding rather than reacting to the student. Making full use of silence, pausing and gesture. Keeping to a natural communicative rhythm of address and response, give and take, push and pull.
Space for student in-put	Providing formats through which students can present and re-present themselves, their companies, jobs and products. Making 'needs-analysis' a format for student presentations. Using the Cuisenaire format.
Mental and emotional space	Keeping planning skeletal. Leaving space in your mind to focus on the student. Knowing which feelings you regard as 'improper' in one-to-one.
Space for listening	Using and teaching 'auditing' skills: auditing pronunciation features, transcripts, signals and discourse moves. Feeding back your own awareness of your student's signals and discourse. Encouraging 'passive' listening.
Student . learning space	Thinking in terms of degrees of learner independence rather than 'level'. Discussing and negotiating the options at each stage. Allowing the student time to work alone, and being prepared to leave the room.
Imaginative space	Letting the non-verbal imagery (including recollected and anticipated situations) evoked by any activity be your guide to its value. Using techniques such as eliciting imagery, and projective identification.
Space for recollection	Using the time immediately after a lesson to inwardly recollect and review your interaction with the student—on the unspoken as well as the spoken level.

5. Further Techniques and Options

In one-to-one teaching, however, specialised, the technical repertoire of the teacher is more important than the materials repertoire.

In contrast to over-prepared teacher-controlled input the one-to-one teacher's basic strategy is to create space for student input, whilst at the same time working with the student to pre-formulate and re-formulate the material content provided by the student.

Within the basic strategy provided by reformulation however, the teacher needs a wide variety of technical options to help the student to 'audit' effectively and practise the language forms which the teacher feeds in.

On the following pages techniques are presented which serve both the basic strategy and which also help us to respond to as wide a range of individual learning needs and skill requirements as possible.

1. **Formatted pages**
2. **Working with dialogues**
3. **Presentations**
4. **Active reading and listening**
5. **Cards**
6. **Rods**
7. **Dictation**
8. **Drills**
9. **Reading aloud**
10. **Your own language**
11. **Words, gestures and actions**
12. **Graphs**
13. **The student's mother tongue (L1)**
14. **Student visits—a check list**
15. **Check list of techniques and options**
16. **Timetabling and course structure: the basic methodological issues.**

1. Formatted pages

If we simply dive into teaching without probing the student's professional situation and needs we are not doing our job. If, on the other hand, we spend too long simply discussing needs and objectives, we will not be seen to be doing our job.

The registration forms that students fill in when applying to do a one-to-one course are an example of a 'formatted page'. The emphasis is on the information they draw from the student. But they also contain *language*.

Registration forms are filled in prior to the commencement of the course. But the 'needs analysis' is not just a prelude to teaching but can be used *for* teaching. Through it we find out about the student's professional situation and language needs. Meeting and working with a teacher *is* a social and professional situation, requiring the student to communicate the main outlines of his or her own personal and professional world and responsibilities.

The registration form contains language that is pre-formulated for response, for filling-in rather than use. The examples of formatted pages that follow show how pre-formulated language can be supplied for use by the student in describing his or her own job and professional language needs.

They therefore fulfil two functions:

— To draw from the student the sort of information we need in order to tailor our teaching to the individual
— To do this communicatively, and as an overt exercise in presenting and practising language.

The object is to unite our own desire to learn as much about the student as possible with the student's desire to be taught and to learn.

To begin with, even a blank piece of paper suffices:

- Student writes in diary form an account of a typical day in his or her working life (L1 or L2).
- Student presents this account orally (L1 or L2).
- Teacher reformulates in L2 at each stage.
- Student records in reformulated language.
- Student transcribes recording or corrects and elaborates his or her written work from playback.

Options

- Begin with reading and correcting a former student's diary.
- Begin with reading a native-speaker diary eg from the Sunday Times Colour Supplement series 'A Life in the Day of . . .'
- Begin with transcription or note-taking from a recorded description of a daily routine.
- Record a full dialogue, including teacher questions, prompts and responses.
- Teacher reformulates student's presentation in writing.

Alternatively, have the student describe his appointments over the coming week or month using pages from a diary or Personal Organiser. You may be surprised what you can learn.

A Formatted Diary page

Week planner	
	MONDAY

Phone

Write

See

Do

Cash Due	To Pay

Notes

8
– 30 –
9
– 30 –
10
– 30 –
11
– 30 –
12
– 30 –
1
– 30 –
2
– 30 –
3
– 30 –
4
– 30 –
5
– 30 –
6
– 30 –
7
– 30 –
8
– 30 –
9

Further techniques and options

Needs analysis

'Needs-analysis' in one-to-one can be looked at in three phases:

- what you know about the student before the first day.
- what you find out on meeting the student for the first time.
- what you learn after working with the student for some time.

The official information you obtain before day 1, even if it includes things like tests or a tape of the student, will only give you a picture of his or her 'official' requirements. For example, to speak English with suppliers or customers, to write monthly reports, to entertain visitors, etc. Tests and tapes may give clues as to level, grammatical weaknesses, pronunciation difficulties and so on.

What you find out on meeting the student for the first time may add invaluable detail to this information and include profiles of interlocutors, situations and the student's exact job and responsibilities. Much of this may be so taken for granted by the student that it needs to be prized out, for he or she may be totally unaware of its relevance to the teacher and to the teaching. Needs analysis in this phase has a direct communicative and teaching purpose . . . to make the *student* aware of his or her own needs. This can take a day or a week.

The 'needs-analysis' charts that follow are formatted with this in mind. The idea is to 'brainstorm' the student for the lexis necessary to define needs, to introduce the idea of language functions to the student, and to draw from him or her both detailed information and decisions about priorities. The result is a Scattergram on a sheet of paper or on the board, on which important items are ringed, and then ranked and further described in space below.

This format is not indispensable and the same sort of information can be drawn from informal discussion with the student. This will not, however, necessarily do the same job in making the student aware of the specificity of his or her needs. Even a lot of business students have never heard of 'Business English'.

When student and teacher meet for the first time the only thing the student is committed to is the financial arrangement with the school or with the teacher. The business contract has been sealed, but the educational contract has not even been drawn up. The student knows how much he or she has paid or will have to pay in money. The student does not know what is or will be expected of him or her in the learning process, and what to expect from it.

One possibility for the first day is to draw up such a contract with the student, establishing agreed objectives as well as conditions for successful cooperation. This could be the first thing on the formal *agenda* for the day.

Alternatively, or in addition, information can be given to the students in writing or by the Director of Studies that goes some way towards defining the educational 'contract' with the students. This is necessary in any professional one-to-one relationship and in most cases except one-to-one language teaching it is already more or less clear. When you go to a doctor, accountant, or consultant you know what is expected and what to expect. The boundaries and overlap of personal and professional responsibility are reasonably clear, and need to be, even though you will spend far less time with any of these professionals than, say, with a one-to-one tutor on an intensive language course.

This issue becomes important in the final phase of 'needs-analysis'. What the teacher learns about the student after working together for some time, and vice versa—what the student learns about the teacher or the teaching—may put the initial 'contract' in question. This simply means that student and teacher discover each other as people. Paper images and official 'needs' give way to the flesh-and-blood personality and the true motivation of the student. The student's professional needs may or may not be identical to his or her individual *desires* and *interest* in learning a language.

We cannot complain about a student's lack of interest or 'motivation' if we do not respond to individual propensities, desires and interests as well as to objective 'needs'. Desire and interest are the true motivators, as well as enjoyment, fun, and a sense of success. Needs by themselves, however well-defined and well-met, cannot be relied upon to motivate.

The third phase of needs-analysis, therefore, transcends needs-analysis and aims at a balance, or if possible, a fusion, of the student's objective needs and subjective desires. This is where the imagination, interests and intuition of the teacher can play their full role in making the course a success and a rewarding experience for teacher and student. It may also require a conscious and open re-negotiation of objectives, methods or topics with the student, based on what the teacher has sensed or learned rather than just assumed or been told.

There is an additional, fourth, phase to needs-analysis, and that is assessment. Here again it is the subjective element that counts. At all stages in teaching the student's subjective assessment of his or her own progress actually contributes to that progress or to the lack of it.

At the end of a course the student should also be in a position to make his or her own objective assessment of further needs. To rely on outside assessments and assessors is itself a sign of insecurity and lack of linguistic self-awareness. The teacher's role remains the same: to provide the student with a format and with the language necessary to express his or her feelings and assess his or her progress. In contrast, it is not the teacher's job to 'prove' improvement to the student or anyone else.

Ways of using a needs-analysis chart

A needs-analysis chart is more than a pre-course piece of information. It can be used in the teaching, particularly early in the course, in a variety of ways:

- Format pages along similar lines to those which follow, and prepare copies
- Elicit needs-defining lexis from the student
- Build up a 'scattergram' of items on paper and on whiteboard if possible
- Discuss possibilities for sorting the items into groups
- Student identifies and rings items relevant to his or her needs
- Student selects the four most important items and ranks these in order of priority, giving additional details in writing
- Language modelling and practice, for example:
     I mainly need English for ...
     ... is the first priority as I see it.
     I'd like to get practice in ......ing .

WHO WILL YOU BE SPEAKING TO ?

names?   position?   friends?
    manufacturers?   customers ?
job?   company?   status?
    superiors ?   clients?
accent?   nationality?
    subordinates?   suppliers?
    relationship to you?   dialect?

YOUR NEEDS	DETAILS
1	
2	
3	
4	

IMPORTANT SITUATIONS YOU WILL FACE

place? frequency? audience?
time? subject? past experience?
your role?
preparation
purpose?
WHY? WHEN? WHERE? HOW OFTEN?
BEFORE? WHO? WHAT?

YOUR NEEDS	DETAILS
1	
2	
3	
4	

Further techniques and options

Similar charts can be made for the following, using the suggested key words and others the reader may care to add. In each case it is best to open the possibilities by adding two or three question marks.

Communicative needs

I need English for . . .

meetings	tourism
travel	negotiations
conferences	secretarial tasks
attending lectures	giving presentations
examinations	academic study
social conversation	? ? ? ? ?

Language skills

Speaking	*Listening*	*Reading*	*Writing*
presentations	training	newspapers	telexes
meetings	lectures	letters	reports
one-to-one	radio	reports	note-taking
telephone	instructions	manuals	letters
? ? ?	? ? ?	? ? ?	? ? ?

Things I need to do in English

argue	greet and introduce people
discuss proposals	express an opinion
confirm information	answer questions
criticise and complain	compare and contrast
request and offer	make small talk
describe processes	verbalise figures and graphs
advise and suggest	interrupt and make points

describe— people, jobs, products, places . . .

Things I can do already (but need additional practice)

count	shop	give personal details
spell	use a phone box	ask for directions
read a menu	tell the time	buy tickets—train, theatre, etc.
change money	book a hotel	make appointments on the phone
? ? ? ?	? ? ? ?	? ? ? ?

Language needs

The English of . . .

banking	marketing	finance
accountancy	economics	import/export
advertising	medicine	sales
computers	tourist trade	retail trade
electronics	personnel management	the . . . industry
? ? ? ?	? ? ? ?	? ? ? ?

Remember the person who deals with bank advertising, or marketing computers to the retail trade needs to reveal real language needs by a matrix combining several items in this list, together with items from several other lists. The objective is to help the student to specify his/her needs as clearly as possible.

Resources

host family	radio	walkman
cassettes	textbooks	company materials
answer keys	newspapers	TV
manuals	specialist journals	pens- multi-colour,
reference books:	dictionaries:	erasable, markers
phrase books	monolingual	stationery:
grammar books	bilingual	files
business books	technical	document wallets
(non EFL)	business	cards
		card index
		"address book"

The one-to-one teacher has several over-lapping roles, one of which is to guide the student in the management of his or her learning. The provision of useful resources is essential, and teachers should not necessarily assume that every student will have thought about this. A discussion early in the course can help the student to work more efficiently, and keep more useful records.

Teacher's summary

Finally, the teacher will need to summarise the findings of the various student scattergrams under headings such as:

Important situations facing the student
Things the student can do already
Basic communicative needs
Functions of English to be covered
Language skills
Specialised lexical and language needs
Key people student will be using English with (and medium)
Resources

The basic idea is simple—if the teacher is to respond to the individual one-to-one student, a considered programme of needs-analysis should *form part of the actual teaching programme.*

Pre-formulation using partial scripts

An alternative format to the needs-analysis charts, particularly for use on day one, is a partial script providing space for student input in the form of:

1. Multiple choice completion of sentence 'heads'

2. Open sentences for completion by student

3. Graphical or tabular formats for verbalisation by student

In other words the student is provided with 'function' words and inputs the 'content' or vice versa.

The multiple-choice statements can be used to teach or test vocabulary and grammar:

> *the managing director*
> *I'm an engineer*
> *a secretary*

Further techniques and options

Open sentences highlight features of syntax and word order:

$$I \text{ need English for } \begin{array}{l} \textit{(my job)} \\ \textit{(writing reports)} \end{array}$$

In addition we can introduce multiple choice sentence heads:

$$I \begin{array}{l} \textit{need} \\ \textit{don't need} \end{array} \textit{help in learning the terminology of} \ldots$$

Graphical and tabular formats allow a wider range of language possibilities to be presented at a glance.

The models that follow are examples only (see page 89), intended for executive students. You might like to consider how it could be improved or altered to suit your students. Formats can be tailored in advance or even devised in lesson time and dictated to the student.

Circles

On pages 93 and 94 there are two interlocking circle diagrams. These, too, are formatted pages which encourage, and provide a shape for student input. Such simple means are a great help in providing a framework, and thus a structure, for student input.

Student assessment sheets

In a similar way, one-to-one lends itself particularly to involving the student in assessing the progress and success of the course. Such assessments can be valuable in helping to re-define the course objectives and methods continuously throughout the whole teaching period. Again, however, students may require some initial guidance in establishing a suitably wide range of criteria. Then, if the assessment is to be performed efficiently, most students will find a pre-designed format helpful.

Here is a range of possible criteria, and on page 96 a simple possible student evaluation sheet.

Teaching results

It is usually thought that the purpose of a lesson or course is something that can be determined at the start. The success of the student is then measured in relation to this pre-defined purpose. This ignores the fact that the relation between purpose and result is always asymptotic. According to the Oxford Dictionary this means "Approaching nearer and nearer to a given curve but without actually meeting it within a finite distance". The distance in short intensive courses is finite indeed. Accordingly we must evaluate and reckon results in different terms. I propose two definitions of this result.

1. The result of a course or lesson is the meaning it has for the student.

2. To be more precise: the result is the result.
   By this I mean that the result may not be what we intended but may still be a positive result. The result has to be looked for and not just 'measured' in terms defined by our goal, plan or purpose. Only by looking for, and finding the real result, can we learn to plan our teaching according to the real and not the putative or formal goals. Sometimes these are closely related. In a lot of cases the relationship is asymptotic and, above all, unpredictable. In one-to-one we cannot

ignore the fact that different students not only respond differently but learn differently from the same activity.

Possible results are far more varied than simple improvement in the student's 'level of English' (however that could be defined!). We may well also want to consider improvements in some or all of the following:

awareness	register familiarity
accuracy	naturalness in speech
fluency	discourse sensitivity
vocabulary	range of response
confidence	situational management
speech clarity	use of functions
listening ability	use of structures
motivation	use of idioms
passive knowledge	cultural familiarity
active knowledge	resource utilisation
understanding	self-access capability
learning ability	analytic skills
independence	observation skills
conversational responsiveness	identification skills
preparedness	

What results do you observe?

Make your own list of indices of progress and turn this into a chart for continuous assessment or beginning/end assessment of your student.

	marginal increase	significant increase
index 1		
index 2		
index 3		

Compare assessments with other teachers and offer the student the opportunity for self-assessment using the same wide range of indices. Ask your student to rank these in order of importance.

Procedure for use of partial script

- Lead in through student's in-tray after initial introduction, conversation and diagnostic discussion with student.
- Work through the pages informally, making notes and checking student's basic vocabulary, pronunciation and grasp of structures. For beginners or elementary students use to teach. No student writing.

Further techniques and options

- Once the student is comfortable with the contents and language of the format switch to an interview mode in which student uses the format as basis for his or her responses to a series of teacher questions. Teacher completes a separate copy of the format in writing. Interview recorded.

- Return to an informal, discussion mode, this time focusing on question formation, for each item on the format in turn.

- Alternatively, simply replay recording of interview and ask/help the student to transcribe the teacher's questions. This gives the student his or her first lesson in really listening to teacher talk and learning from it.

- Student can also use the recording to compare his or her own oral presentation or responses with the corrected transcript of these completed by the teacher during the interview: transcription as a self-correction exercise.

- In addition you may wish to focus, not on question formation alone, but on the teacher's responses to student statements. Responses such as 'I see', 'Mm', 'Really', 'Do you', etc., which are both simple and essential aspects of English discourse for all students to become aware of and begin to adopt.

- Present student with a typed copy of question sheet for auditing pronunciation features, including intonation, from 'dictation' by teacher. Or ask the student to conduct the teacher's reading of these questions until they sound right with respect to intonation and stress.

- Interview mode again. This time the student asks the questions and completes another copy of the format from teacher responses. This is a good place for the empty chair technique. Student addresses questions to an imaginary student in the empty chair. Teacher answers for that student. Record this interview too and focus on responses to statements rather than questions.

- Alternatively use a recording of an interview with another student as an exercise in 'aural gap-filling'. Recording is played and student completes the format with details of the other student. Remember to give student control of the cassette-corder.

- Student summarises information obtained from the interview/recording by reading the completed format in the 3rd person.

My name's _____

I'm from _____ in _____

My address is _____
My telephone number is _____.

I'm the President   of . . .
           Managing Director

      the Marketing   Manager for
           Distribution
           Product

      a   Production Control
           Personnel
           Training
           Works
           Sales
           Retail
           Financial

I'm a   Secretary
         Senior Secretary
         Sales Representative
         Sales Engineer
         Technical Sales Representative
         Production Engineer
         Computer Programmer
         Systems Analyst

I'm an   Accountant
         Architect
         Electrical Engineer
         Electronic Engineer
         Office Manager
         Administrator

The full name of my company is _____

_____

I have worked for _____
_____ for _____ months/years.

Further techniques and options

I have been a   the   _____

an

_____ for _____ months/years.

My previous position was _____

_____ for _____

I left this job in _____.

I think I will stay in my present job for another _____ years.

My company produces _____.

It specialises in _____.

It is a subsidiary of _____.

It owns subsidiaries in _____.

It employs _____.

Its headquarters is in _____.

The place I work is _____.

I am responsible for _____.

I am responsible to _____.

My department consists of _____.

I deal mainly with _____.

My tasks are to _____.

My job is   interesting/boring.
             challenging/routine.
             time-consuming.
             rewarding.

The company is doing well at the moment.
                        badly

There is a lot of competition.
      isn't

Good English is useful necessary for my career.
                 vital

The last English course I attended was ___.

I completed this in _____(year).

The English-speaking countries I have visited are _____.

This is my
first
second
third
fourth
time in _____(country).

In my own language I talk a lot/very little.
quickly/slowly.

I enjoy talking about
business.
politics.
sport.
people.
music.
travel.
? ? ?

I know a lot about _____.

I could give a talk on _____.

I have given talks on _____ to _____.

The materials I have brought with me are
_____.

I need English to talk to
Bosses
Clients
Customers
my Colleagues in _____.
our Suppliers
Trainees
Agents
Staff

The most important people I will be speaking to are _____
_____
_____.

My English should be good enough to
   introduce myself
   introduce others
   give a good impression
   exchange small talk
   instruct others
   persuade others
   give presentations
   understand presentations
   speak at meetings
   discuss things one-to-one
   play a role in negotiations
   present or discuss offers
   plan projects
   show people round places
   speak on the phone
   take dictation
   write letters
   make appointments
   book hotels
   write telexes
   write reports/summaries
   translate documents

I can already _____
_____ in English.

In _____ months/years I wish to be able to
_____ in English.

The most important real-life test of my
English in the near future will be _____
_____
_____.

In this course I wish to concentrate on ____
_____.

My social circles

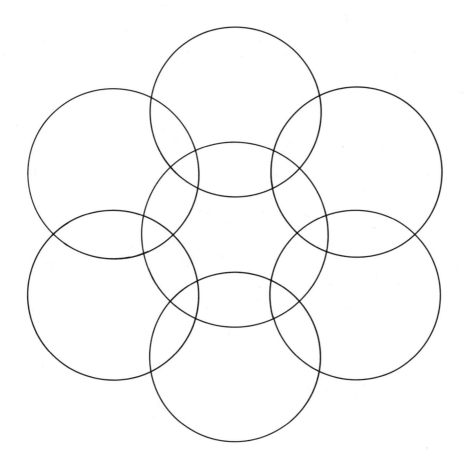

Sign your name or your initials in the centre of the diagram.

Write the initials or first names of all the most important people in your life in the surrounding circles.

- Group them according to something they have in common.
- If a person belongs to more than one group place them in the overlap of two of the circles.
- Place the person closest to you in each of the groups in the overlap with the central circle.
- Find a name or a way of describing each of the circles.
- Discuss the diagram.
  Do all the circles have a common member?
  Which contains the most people?
  Which is most important to you?
  Which represents the past, which the present and which the future?
  Are they all linked to your 'inner circle'?
  Which circle/member do you want to cultivate most?
  Are there people or circles you have forgotten to include?

Further techniques and options

Organisations I belong to:

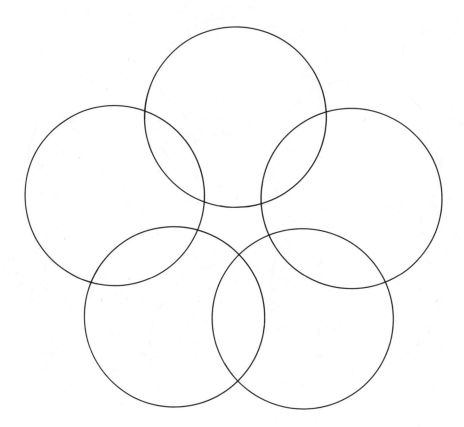

Write in the name or initials of 5 organisations that you belong to.
    Write in the name or initials of the people you know in each of the organizations.
    Write the names or initials of 'link-persons' in the overlaps.
    Discuss as with the social circles.

Partial script for a presentation (see page 102)

I'd like to begin by referring you to ...... pointing out / looking at

As you know / can see ......

Now, during the last year .....

I'm sure you'll recall that last year .....

So we have reason to think .....

On the other hand ......

Sorry, did you want to ask a question?

Right
Yes
I see

If I understand you correctly / Am I right in thinking that you .....

Yes, well in fact .....

This means in turn that .....

So our overall strategy will be to .....

If .....

then .....

If not we will have to .....

Personally I believe that .....

and I'm confident that .....

The essence of the matter, as always is .....

Further techniques and options

SCHOOL LOGO	STUDENT'S EVALUATION SHEET				

Activity	Useful? 1-5	Enjoyable? 1-5	Method of teacher 1-5	Time spent — too little	too much

Suggestions for week 2	Priority listing

2. Working with dialogues

Getting the student to speak or write from a partial script or model format (diary, chart, table etc.) is one example of Preformulation. Instead of pre-teaching the student and expecting a natural language transfer to relevant communicative tasks and situations, we begin with a task and build-in all the language the student will need to fulfil it, in the form of sentence heads, model structures or lists of useful expressions.

Dialogues play a major role in language teaching and the techniques with which we develop or work with them also include Formatting and Preformulation, Auditing and Reformulation.

A basic *format* for dialogue work is itself the formatted page on which each turn in the dialogue is described:

Offer a cigarette	
	Refuse, saying you don't smoke
Ask permission to smoke	
	Give permission and offer an ashtray

Using this format as a starting point we can now either help the student by providing preformulated language, or throw him/her in the deep end and reformulate his/her output; we can pre-teach or post-teach.

Preformulation usually means giving the student a list of expressions or getting him/her to extract such expressions from a recorded dialogue. If the expressions fall into two or more functional categories (eg 'offering' and 'suggesting') you can begin by presenting or dictating a mixed bag of expressions and asking the student to sort them into categories. You can format a page for this purpose:

OFFERS	SUGGESTIONS

Alternatively it is often more interesting and stimulating to begin by playing a recorded dialogue and asking the student to *audit* this for the particular structures or functions with which it is loaded.

In one-to-one we can spend as much as one and a half hours on something like a simple situational dialogue from a standard coursebook, helping the student to grasp *both* the 'gist' *and* the exact words spoken.

What the student hears is not just a matter of his or her so-called 'listening skill' but of the knowledge, expectations and 'search images' that he or she projects on the stream of sound. Grammar and listening are not two different things but go together in the student's ability to reconstruct what was said, anticipate or fill-in missing words, unheard contractions etc.

In a class teaching situation listening comprehension and language analysis are necessarily separated. But some of my most enjoyable lessons in one-to-one have been when I have helped a student to understand a recorded dialogue by thinking about the exact words that could have been spoken, by being prompted to think about possible structures and functions, by listening to form ('auditing') as well as to content. In one-to-one we can follow the natural dialectic of the student's structural knowledge and vocabulary and his or her ability to reconstruct the spoken word. In this way the student quickly registers progress both in learning *to* hear, and in learning *from* hearing.

Now able to transcribe a recorded dialogue without the teacher's help, he or she can also audit the transcript and extract the structures or functions which will be activated in reconstructing it or role playing it.

Reformulation

Even a recorded and closed dialogue can be used as an *open* dialogue. By stopping the tape at each turn and asking the student to anticipate the response of the next speaker, we can invite student input. Or we can ask the student to improvise a dialogue from a skeleton description, record this and then compare it with the published recording. We can also make up our own *open* dialogues, recording them with gaps for student responses, reformulating his or her response before he or she records, and then asking the student to transcribe the whole dialogue, including the reformulated responses. Such teacher-prepared open dialogues can be specifically tailored to the individual student's communicative needs and situation (as telephone dialogues or enquiries for example).

Finally, an entire dialogue can be built up by reformulation. The situation is defined. The student takes either or both parts, suggests lines for each turn. Having suggested a line the teacher reformulates this and the student records the reformulated version. The student then suggests a line for the responding speaker. Having reformulated this, it can then be recorded by either the teacher (if the student is to take one part only) or by the student. The important thing is that the student suggests the language for both parts, for the student knows the *situation* better than the teacher. Either way, the result is an error free recording which the student can then audit and transcribe, learning from the language he or she has already practised in context.

I have said that the skills students need to learn are the very skills that teachers employ in preparing lessons. A good example is working with dialogues.

The starting point provided by the teacher will either be a skeletal format with a functional description of each 'turn' or an actual published recording.

But the skeletal format is itself a use of language (reported speech) and a valuable exercise is to ask the *student* to create such a map of the turns in a social or professional dialogue or negotiation.

Similarly, the alternative to using a published cassette is to make one with the student, allowing him or her to determine its content, and providing, by reformulation, the language appropriate to it. Such a dialogue cannot fail to be specific and relevant to the individual's needs and objectives.

Using Cuisenaire rods and board (see page 120)

The simplest possible format for one-to-one consists of a table and two chairs, a walkman cassette and a box of Cuisenaire rods. The rods, together with a rod board can be used to represent words, functional expressions, or whole lines of dialogue; indeed an entire mini-dialogue. The teacher can use them both to indicate gaps in the student's listening comprehension or to present reformulations of student language before the student records these. The student can use them to represent whatever words he or she hears spoken on the tape, or as a mnemonic for practising the reformulated lines that the teacher provides. Structures and expressions can be laid out as substitution patterns for practice drills, using rods to represent key words or word ending (*-ing, -ed* etc) or used directly as realia. The rods can even be used as puppets representing the people present at a meeting for example, with different colours for different positions of responsibility or known colleagues/clients of the student. In this way an entire meeting can be role-played, with the student taking each part in turn, and the teacher reformulating each turn for the student to record.

With this sort of overall format for one-to-one we avoid the chaos of multiple photocopies from a collection of coursebooks bewildering to both student and teacher.

Reformulation on Day 1

Having conducted an initial fact-finding but informal interview with the student on the first meeting, we can follow this up either with a Preformulated 'partial script' with which the student learns to re-present him or herself, company and needs using appropriate language, set out on a formatted page, *or* we can use reformulation immediately and for the same purpose. That is to say we can put in a blank tape, set our machine to 'record', and tell the student that:

— we wish to summarise the facts by recording a formal interview

— we wish him or her to give a 5 minute presentation on his/her job or company

— we are going to record a conversation

Whichever option or way of putting it we choose, the idea is now to reformulate whatever the student says at a level one degree above his or her performance level, and to get the student to record in chunks, not at the first go, but only *after,* and *following,* our reformulation. If an interview or conversation mode is chosen, this should be simple. If a presentation mode is selected, or if the student finds it difficult to stop talking, it may be necessary to interrupt gently in order to create an interval for reformulation and recording.

Alternatively, the teacher may simply take notes on the students output for a 'retrospective' replay and reformulation of the whole presentation.

CLL Dialogues

Community Language Learning is a bilingual approach to teaching in which the teacher serves as counsellor/informer whispering to the student the words they need in L2 to say whatever they feel moved to say in the immediate reality of the group. This they communicate to the teacher privately. The product of CLL is a tape-transcript of a dialogue conducted entirely in L2. The words have been put into the students mouths, but what the students are *saying* with these words is not. This is the converse of the usual situation in which the student has to find the right words but what is to be said and done through these words is imposed by the theme of the lesson and does not arise spontaneously as authentic communication.

CLL thus fulfills the twin criteria of:
- creating space for student input
- allowing authentic communication to occur.

It's use in one-to-one requires that the teacher can understand the student's L1. In the past this was no problem since teachers tended to be native L1 speakers rather than 'foreigners', with all the advantages that this can present. For a sizeable minority of teachers this is still true, but in many schools there will be enough linguistic competence in various foreign languages around to allocate teachers to students according to the foreign language skills of the former. Some schools indeed, only take students from or within a certain country. Here especially, one-to-one teachers should be selected according to their familiarity with their students language as well as their general teaching skills and qualifications.

Applying CLL in one-to-one is very simple. A focus for discussion is taken or a role play set up. Then:
- The student says something in L1
- The teacher translates
- The student practices in L2
- The student records (both his or her contribution and the teacher's response).

The dialogue can be replayed bit by bit, offering the student a chance to recall, transcribe and learn from his or her L2 utterances, or re-enacted and studied from a complete transcript typed by the teacher.

Basically then, it is a bilingual version of Reformulation. The great benefit for the teacher is that he or she has a chance to learn the student's real language as this expresses itself in L1. Rather than having to interpret what this language is from guesswork, the teacher discovers what it is by interpreting for the student. The benefit for the student is that the language provided by the teacher is truly 'tailor made' for him or her to communicate real meaning, to *say things with words* rather than simply speak them.

Pre-formatted dialogue page with student turns omitted

3. Presentations

Many one-to-one students are involved in presenting—their company, their products or some special feature of their work. These may include oral presentations, supported by graphics, charts etc, or by written presentations, in the form of reports, brochures, product descriptions etc. Although every presentation is different, as it depends so much on the particular content, the presentation is itself a format, and accordingly provides an appropriate means of practice in one-to-one teaching.

There are several features of presentation preparation which are of particular interest to language teachers:

1. Teachers frequently emphasise the whole before the parts (the essay before the paragraph, the conversation before the necessary linking words to connect one utterance to another). For many business people, a full-blown presentation is the final product of an extensive sales conference, or other long period of preparation which involves many ideas being discussed before being rejected. Here is a model to help language teachers. In preparing a presentation, a student will use, and *need* to use, a great deal of language which is useful in his specific field, but may ultimately be rejected from the particular final product of the exercise—the outline of a particular presentation.

2. Teachers often ask for completeness and coherence too quickly. The ability to prepare and plan a presentation or essay necessarily precedes the ability to produce one!

3. Even more specifically, teachers often forget the central role of lexis in communication. There are good theoretical grounds for thinking that we frequently form our ideas first in words, and only "grammaticalise" if the words alone will not communicate our meaning. Many students undertaking a one-to-one course who are, for example, already active as managers, are frequently required to use English which is simply beyond their present level in the language. One of their principal needs is an inventory of words, or more exactly lexical items, which are central to the subject they wish to discuss.

Planning a presentation in the way described below, means that students *start* without the inhibition of having to grammaticalise, by simply *gathering* the necessary central lexical items.

These items are then *grouped,* a process which itself suggests certain grammatical relationships.

They are also then *sequenced,* another process which suggests certain grammatical relationships. For all these reasons, it is easy to see how preparing a presentation has a central role to play in one-to-one language teaching.

The sequence of blackboard or flip chart visuals and summaries below shows the stages in preparing a presentation. In this particular case, the presentation is itself about making presentations, so that the visuals present a number of ideas which may help teachers to think more clearly about the value of this technique.

1. Gathering ideas

2. Grouping

(scattergram 1 — Gathering ideas)

scripts
overhead projector
key points
clarity
graphs
Core statements in full
economy
notes
Visual aids
sequencing
keywords
introductory and concluding statements
diagrams
vertical scripts
breath voice gesture
auto-dictation
miming delivery
charts
eye contact

(scattergram 2 — Grouping)

PREPARATORY
VISUAL AIDS
5 central statements
cards
diagrams
vertical script
sequencial notes
Video charts
sentence beginnings
whiteboard
flip chart
opening and closing statements
OHP
VDU

SUPPLEMENTARY
Handouts
Samples
summaries
transcripts
literature
books

3. Sequencing

1. Preparation
- build up scattergram with student
- student sorts into groups of key points
- student sequences key points and prepares visual aids
- student composes core sentences with useful language provided by teacher
- student formulates/re-formulates using partial script or list of phrases

2. Rehearsal
- student evaluates a video presentation or presentation by teacher
- student practises marking text for pronunciation, and dividing into breath groups, marking pauses
- student mimes delivery

3. Delivery
- record or video?
- prepare evaluation sheets for teacher and student
- focus on speechwork, gesture, pausing and use of aids

4. Necessary language

I'd like to begin by ......ing
Let me begin with a question:
It's certainly a pleasure to be able to ......
I'm delighted to have the opportunity to ......

Let's look firstly at ......
Now the main advantage, as I see it is ......

As you know ......
As you can see ......
As you will appreciate ......

5. Preparing delivery   6. Other factors to consider

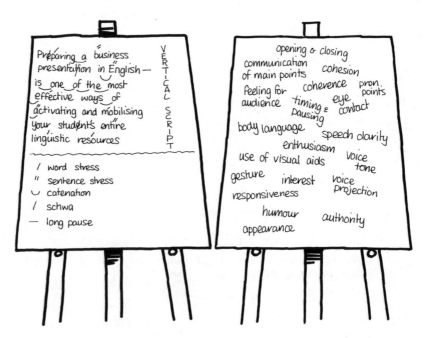

Preparing a business
presentation in English —
is one of the most
effective ways of
activating and mobilising
your students entire
linguistic resources

V E R T I C A L   S C R I P T

/ word stress
" sentence stress
∪ catenation
/ schwa
— long pause

opening & closing
communication   cohesion
of main points
feeling for   coherence   pron.
audience   timing &   eye   points
          pausing   contact
body language   speech clarity
          enthusiasm
use of visual aids   voice
                    tone
gesture   interest   voice
responsiveness   projection
     humour   authority
appearance

As soon as continuous text is committed to paper, particularly if it is typed or printed, it becomes hallowed in a very special way. For this reason, a lot of conventional language teaching's "written homework" can frequently be counter-productive. Once a fair copy has been produced by the student, both teacher and student expect it to be "corrected", which, if this results in it being covered in red ink, can be a very inhibiting process. It is therefore helpful to allow the one-to-one student to work on the blackboard, or better still with a pen on a large paper flip-chart. Both of these mediums suggest that what is written is only provisional—the emphasis is on a process, not on the final product.

If you want to work while sitting at a desk, students should still be encouraged to start by scribbling randomly, as in the charts on the previous two pages, rather than producing carefully prepared lists.

If a student is to make a presentation, we begin by inviting the student to put on the board the *why, what, who* and *how* of the presentation. Presentations serve many different purposes, and if, as teachers, we are to provide the student with the language appropriate to a particular purpose, it is important to negotiate with the student in order to ensure that the purpose is clearly understood. The preparation of a presentation as part of a one-to-one course, partly serves as preparation for similar presentations in the student's professional life. Here is a summary of some of the basic parameters which may be listed by the student as part of their answers to the **wh—** questions above.

Why?   To tell, sell, or impel?
          Purpose?
          Message?

What?   Demonstration/description/report/analysis/promotion/
           explanation/lecture or seminar/training session?

Who?   What do they know?
          What do they expect?
          Likely attitudes?
          Likely questions?

How?   Long?
          Will you deliver?
          Will you prepare?
          Will you remember the words?

Possible topics for a student presentation

Company organisation and subsidiaries
            history
            growth
            policy

Marketing strategy

Product range
            descriptions

New products
Best-selling products
Product development

Further techniques and options

Market share

Results and projections

Personal career history
Career objectives
Position and contribution to company

Sales organisation
    strategy, training

Market trends
Managerial style

Negotiations in hand
Future negotiations

Reports (eg past year)

Describing colleagues (introductions and profiles)

The competition
The customers

Timetable for next month

Economic and political climate in home country
Environmental issues
Teach the teacher your job: responsibilities
                         product information
                         people information
                         briefing for negotiations
                         advice

Advertising

4. Active reading and listening

I have defined "auditing" as all those activities which help to heighten the student's awareness of particular language forms. These activities are not usually seen as associated with macro-skills such as reading or listening, but with micro skills—checking for particular features of the language used.

Though students are exposed to language through the use of text or a tape, there are many things which can be done which concentrate on particular language features, rather than global understanding. These are, in the first instance, based on asking the students to *identify* a particular language feature. Some of the things which can be a focus for student attention while listening or reading are given below.

On the following pages (pages 109 to 113) I have tried to list a wide range of activities all of which come under the general heading of auditing; some will be familiar, some may seem eccentric. The point is simple—one-to-one teaching involves the teacher responding, and varying his or her response, to each individual student, frequently throughout a course. The wider the range of possibilities at the teacher's disposal, the more likely he or she is to find something which will fit the particular needs of an individual student at a certain time. It goes without saying that teachers must choose those activities from the list which are most appropriate to their individual students.

Things the student can be asked to identify on listening or reading:

* words or phrases that are not understood
                    understood but unfamiliar
                    familiar but not understood

Of these, the second group are probably the most important even though emphasis is usually placed on the first. We wish to help the student to acquire language which he or she understands but doesn't 'pick up'. The problem is that students don't listen to form unless they have problem with content. Conversely if the meaning is clear they do not pay any attention to the words that are used.

* collocations, either verb-noun collocations:
                    to quote a price
                    to enter a market

          or adjective-noun collocations:
                    . . . a well-established firm
                    . . . an impressive record

* complex nouns:
                    eg *industrial relations tribunal*
                    manufacturing industry
                    market research

* words with a common root:
                    economy economist economic economical
                    politics politician political

Further techniques and options

- lexical families:

$$concept$$
$$advertising$$
$$campaign \qquad media$$
$$budget$$
$$sales$$
$$agency$$

These can be sorted into groups or collocational pairs.

- references to past, present or future time

    The student can be asked to sort references to the past, for example, into groups, and then compare these groups. In other words to identify verb forms and discover their role, without first being 'taught' them.

- short responses
- opening phrases

    The student can be asked to list and then sort these according to Functions of language, without first naming these functions. He or she can then go on to rank them (eg ranking degrees of agreement or disagreement) and to select those he or she would like to adopt and feels comfortable in using. Let the customer choose the language he or she wants to use! If you think particular language suits an individual, then by all means try to sell it, but the customer has the final word!

Procedure

1. Texts: Student scans, identifies and writes down items
Tapes: Student stops tape on hearing example of a certain type of language, repeats and writes down.

2. Having listed items of the same sort student then sorts the items within the list into groups, and/or ranks them

    eg sorting time references into tenses
       sorting openers into functional groups
       sorting verb-noun collocations into those with or without a
       prepositional verb or an indirect object
       collocations with the same verb or noun

3. Student and teacher agree on definition of the groups and compare them in context eg analysing to discover reason for use of different tenses, responses or structures.

4. Student enters items considered most 'user-friendly' into his or her notebook and considers ways in which he or she could use them.

Summary of steps

Identification
Listing
Sorting or ranking
Naming, comparison and analysis
Selection and transfer

- Following these steps through for a wide variety of language points provides an excellent basis for student reconstruction or role play of the text or dialogue.

> eg student summarises
> eg student and teacher role play
> eg teacher stops tape at turn-intervals and asks student to respond
>   instead of recorded speaker

It is important to remember that the objective is to heighten the student's awareness of language forms, as well as meaning. The emphases are on this increased awareness of particular items, on making the student's passive language active, and on a generally more acute and accurate observation of language for the student.

Auditing tapes

The purpose of these activities is to help the student observe spoken text more carefully.

Listening visualisation

- Listen and form a picture of the place
  eg a hotel: remember the last time you were in a hotel.
    What did it look like inside?
- Listen and form a picture of the speakers (from the tone of voice)
  eg sex, age, appearance, height, dress, gestures

Listening identification

- Listen and imagine you are there: where are you sitting/standing, what can you see? what are you doing there?
- Listen and identify with one of the speakers: where are you sitting/ standing? how are you feeling? what gestures do you make? who are you facing and what expression are you making?

Listening anticipation, recollection, and response

Teacher stops tape at various points or uses a paused or open dialogue:

- Listen and repeat the speaker's last words
- Listen and anticipate the speaker's next words
- Listen and respond to the speaker

These are good ways of auditing complete as well as open dialogues.

Mental recollection, anticipation, and response

- Listen and imagine yourself responding in the pauses
- Listen and visualize a speaker responding in the pauses
- Listen and hear a speaker responding in the pauses

What does (s)he say? How does (s)he say it? How is (s)he sitting, standing, feeling, looking? What gestures/expressions does the speaker have?

- Listen again and see if you want to change your picture.
- Listen again and identify with another speaker.
- Listen, identify with a speaker and anticipate the next speaker's response.
- Listen and imagine an alternative response.

Further techniques and options

Active listening

Students are used to the idea of listening in order to understand—their main attention is on the *content* of what is said. For this reason they often do not listen to anything else. One-to-one provides an ideal opportunity to widen their range of listening skills, making them more aware of how language is used. This is an extension of the auditing procedures we have already discussed.

Students can, for example, be asked to signal by making a hand movement whenever:

- they don't hear something properly
- they don't understand something
- there is a pause
- a speaker hesitates
- they think they could interrupt the speaker
- the speaker's voice rises
- there is a difference between the tape and the text
- they hear
    —a past tense verb
    —a third person-**s**
    —an -**ing** form
    —a request being made
    —the word **well**
    —a rising intonation
    —a question
    —one speaker acknowledging another etc.

Listening comprehension

Again, a range of skills can be identified more than simply "understanding". Here is a short list of possibilities:

- Listen and ask one question
- Listen and remember one thing/word/phrase
- Listen and answer these questions
- Listen and re-tell in your own words
- Listen and take notes
- Listen and identify the feelings expressed by the speakers
- Listen and describe the scene/speakers
- Listen and fill the gaps/complete the sentences with your own words
- Listen and complete the story/dialogue in your own words
- Listen and complete the graph/table/chart/diagram/questionnaire

Transcription

Transcription is the process by which the student listens to the tape and makes or uses a written copy of the taped material. A number of activities are possible, the simplest being, of course, that the student listens and transcribes—another example of re-formatting as we have discussed earlier. There are however, a number of other possibilities each aimed at helping the student to audit the tape, heightening awareness of specific language features in the taped material.

- Listen and mark the stresses/schwas/pauses/intonation on the text
- Listen and correct the errors in the text from the tape or *vice versa*
- Listen and do a graph of the intonation pattern
- Listen and do a graph of the rise and fall of the speaker(s) voice(s) or of my voice

Recording

- Listen and practise your own responses to the speaker(s) on the tape: then listen and record your responses in the intervals

Passive listening

- Listen only to the sounds of the language
- Listen only to the music/background noises
- Listen only to the rise and fall of my own/the speaker(s) voices
- Try not to listen

The last may appear a curious suggestion but if in doubt, the reader is invited to try it! Some of us may have difficulty in remembering things, but that does not mean it is easy for us to forget certain things which we would, perhaps, rather forget. This is a similar case—if the student can be encouraged to try not to listen, what in fact happens is that they listen in a different way and, while relaxed, for some students at least, certain features of the listening are more acutely observed subconsciously.

Auto-dictation

- Read or listen to the words/phrases/turns one at a time:
  Think the meaning/message
  Hear yourself speaking them
  Write them down
  Check your transcription

Auto-enactment

- Read or listen to the turns in the dialogue
- Think of a gesture/movement/expression appropriate
- Mime the lines silently
- Mouth the words silently
- Mime and mouth or whisper the words
- Say the words out aloud in the manner of your movements, gestures and expressions.

Language laboratory

- Repeat the words on tape and compare with the speaker
- Repeat and record your words in the intervals and compare with the speaker.

Further techniques and options

Auditing texts

These activities help the student observe written text more carefully.

Scanning

- Find a word or phrase which means ......
- Find a word or phrase used to request/suggest/offer something
- Find a word or phrase through which the speaker confirms that (s)he is listening
- Underline all verbs referring to past time

Gap-filling

- Fill in the missing words
- Fill in the missing preposition
- Fill in the verbs in the correct form

Correction

- Cross out all the unnecessary words
- Correct the errors

Jigsaw reconstruction

- Arrange the extracts/turns/sentences in their correct order
- Number the extracts/turns/sentences in their correct order

Information gap

- Find out from me what you need to know to complete the text/table sentences/article

Information transfer

- Transfer the information from text to chart or vice versa
- Write a summary/letter/report based on the information in the text
- Reorganise the information under the following headings

Comprehension

- True/False discrimination of statements
- Multiple choice identification of meaning
- Identification of missing information
- Judgement, evaluation and decision-making based on text

Reading aloud

- Correcting errors or filling gaps
- With emphasis on speech work for addressing an audience
- In a different tense/person

Comparing

- Two or more examples of the same type of text (eg adverts)
- The same text presented in different registers

Visualisation

- Reading dialogue and forming a picture of the situation and speakers

Guessing

- Reading and guessing the meaning of words from context
- Reading and substituting appropriate words for others not understood
- Reading and guessing the meaning of nonsense words from context

Listing

- Items of vocabulary, conjunctions, prepositions
- References to the past or future

Sorting lists

- Sorting references to past time into *(have)* plus participle and simple past forms
- Sorting into nouns, verbs, adjectives etc

Further techniques and options

5. Cards

I emphasised earlier the importance of creating space, and where possible, choosing small teaching aids. Library cards certainly have their uses but it is possible to buy blank (on both sides) playing cards. These are a pleasant quality of card, and a convenient size for the student. They are available, in packs of 1000 from E. J. Arnold, Parkside Lane, Dewsbury Rd., Leeds LS11 5TD (Telephone 772112, Telex 556347).

For most students cards are a familiar aid to learning. At the simplest level there is the lexical card set with a word in L2 on one side and the L1 equivalent on the other. Students can test their recall by going through the set one card at a time, with either the L1 or the L2 side face up. If they make a mistake or have difficulty with a particular item, the relevant card should not be replaced at the bottom of the pack but somewhere very near the top, so as to offer an early opportunity to reinforce learning.

Bilingual card sets can be prepared by the student, by the teacher, and by student and teacher working together. They can be extremely helpful not only for revision purposes, but also in providing equivalents for common colloquial expressions, idiomatic phrases in either language, sayings, and technical vocabulary. A student may have heard the expression *It went well/smoothly* a hundred times and still not realise that this phrase is the nearest equivalent to the German verb *klappen* . . . and thus be at a loss.

It is because words in different languages do *not* carry the same connotations, or may even be untranslatable from one language to another, that bilingual equivalents are necessary to 'fill in' for habitual responses in L1. A teacher with some knowledge of the student's L1 can put this to good use. Alternatively textbooks and phrase books for teaching the student's language can be a good source.

Teachers can also prepare revision sets for cards for their students, incorporating not just translation tests but every conceivable type of written exercise:

- Gap-filling exercises with the completed sentence on the flip side
- Graph on one side and verbalisation on the other
- Time-line on one side and sample sentence in the corresponding tense on the other
- Question and answer
  address and response
  statement and tag

The possibilities are endless, and therefore easily exploited to perfectly tailor a set of cards to a particular student's remedial or revision needs.

So far I have not encountered a student who has not been delighted to receive such a set (even though some would be reluctant to prepare one themselves). They are a mark of care and effort on the part of the teacher, and can be useful in remotivating students, reviewing work covered, and reducing the learning task to tangible and manageable proportions.

A tidily-boxed card set is an excellent take-away 'product' at the end of a one-to-one course.

Again, it needs to be emphasised, that rather than the clutter of large textbooks, notebooks, dictionaries etc., in the smaller scale of one-to-one teaching, a collection of cards is frequently a much more user-friendly aid.

In one-to-one especially, cards can be an excellent aid for the teacher as well. The use of cards offers unlimited scope to the teacher's imagination, and the suggestions that follow should not be regarded as definitive.

- bilingual card games
- 'jigsaw' dialogue reconstruction
- word-order practice
- story-telling based on a sequence of nouns or verbs
- say something about yourself using the word or words on card(s) picked at random
- putting keywords from a text or dialogue on cards. Pick a card and recall the passage or line of dialogue.
- cue cards for student presentations
- card conversations between teacher and student in which each must use the word or phrase on his or her card to address or respond to the other
- making a set of pronunciation cards using words to do with a student's job or hobby eg using golfing words as examples of the English vowels
- thinking of examples of different spellings of the same sound or the same spelling for different sounds and recording these on cards
- pronunciation sorting and matching exercises
- sorting cards into groups or matching them in pairs

by pronunciation	by time reference
by tense	by collocation
by aspect	by like or dislike of the word
by notion	by register
by function	by usefulness to the student

  for example, pronunciation:

by final sound	by position of stressed syllable
by number of syllables	by vowel sound
by rhyme	

A number of examples are shown on the following pages. Clearly the cards should be typed or neatly written if they are to be a serious learning aid.

Er hat ein Vogel.

He's nuts.

awkward structures

Qu'est qui ne vas pas ?

What's the matter ?

everyday phrases

N'êtes vous pas M. Ransom?

Aren't you Mr. Ransom ?

idioms

Ltd.

Limited Liability Company
GmbH (Aktien Gesellschaft
mit beschränkter Haftung)

abbreviations

How do you do .

How are you ?

How do you do .
Pleased to meet you.

Fine thanks, and you?
Very well, thank you .

greetings

Is Mr. Carson there ?

-'- - - - - - he isn't.

I'm afraid he isn't .
Can I take a message?

functional expressions

Would you call a taxi for me ?
Would you mind calling a taxi for me?
Would you like a taxi ?
Would you like to go by taxi ?
Would you like me to get you a taxi ?

W_ _ _ call a taxi for me?
W_ _ _ _ calling a taxi for me?
W_ _ _ _ a taxi ?
W_ _ _ _ _ go by taxi ?
W_ _ _ _ _ _ get you a taxi?

uses of "would"

What do you do ?

What are you doing ?

I'm a freelance consultant .

I'm doing a survey for a washing powder company .

grammar examples

1. increased
2. has/have increased
3. was increasing
4. is increasing
5. has been increasing
6. is expected to increase

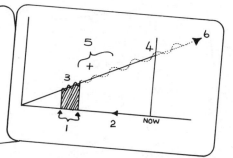

graphical time

1. She's a clever girl.   Is she?
2. She's started school already. _____?
3 She's doing very well. _____?
4 She gets good grades. _____?
5 She can play the piano. _____?
6 She gave a performance last week. _____?

2. Has she
3. Is she
4. Does she
5. Can she
6. Did she

short answers/auxiliaries

increase increased increased
rise —— ——
fall —— ——

rose / risen
fell / fallen

verb forms

θiatə

theatre

phonetics

1. I met him — Peter's party.
2. I'll pick you up — the airport.
3. What time will you arrive — Geneva ?
4. You need to be — the airport — six o'clock.

1. at
2. at
3. in
4. at, by

prepositions

I arrived in London two weeks ago.
+
I am still in London now
= I'_ ____ in London two weeks.

I've been in London two weeks.

grammar concepts

I ~~will~~ to France next year
clue : 1 2

I want to go to France next year.

typical mistakes

We make/do business in the Middle East.

do business

multiple choice

6. Cuisenaire rods

Cuisenaire rods can be used by students in many ways. For example representing his or her family, company, or place of work. The teacher will find it helpful to experiment beforehand, deciding which of the various lengths and colours of rod are most suited for representing or demonstrating the chosen subject, whether to place them upright or lengthwise and so on. Having played around in this way you can model a particular use of the rods for your student, and use this as a way of presenting language. Alternatively this use can be left entirely to the student's imagination.

The benefit of the rods lies in their tangibility, the way that they can involve the student in a physical and imaginative task which gives a visible and concrete shape to the linguistic task. They can also give visibility to sounds, words and sentences as such without recourse to board writing or texts. In this way they serve as a silent and non-verbal aid to memorising words and word order, as well as indicating features of pronunciation.

Two rods touching can indicate linking.

Two one cm rods can represent vowels in a diphthong.

An additional one cm rod can represent an extra syllable. Other examples are given on pages 122/3.

Intonation of an utterance can also be represented using three imaginary lines for three pitch levels along which the rods can be placed.

Of especial value is their use in representing auxiliary verbs, contractions, and verb endings. For example a one cm rod for third person **—s**, two cm for **—ed** and three cm for **—ing.** Another approach is to use slightly longer rods for representing the entire verb in its five basic forms:

1st form	(eg *tell*)	green 3 cm
2nd form	(eg *told*)	purple 4 cm
3rd form	(eg *told*)	purple 4 cm or yellow 5 cm for contrasting past participles
4th form	(eg *telling*)	green 6 cm
5th form	(eg *tells*)	additional 1 cm

In practice any set of conventions that one can establish prove either consistent and incomplete or complete and inconsistent. It is up to the teacher to judge the usefulness of any given representation according to the needs of the moment, whilst at the same time sticking to conventions established for these needs.

Uses of the rods

Use them to represent language items:

- words, patterns and structures
- syllables and morphemes (eg verb endings)
- phonemes or letters
- features of pronunciation (stress, voicing, number of syllables, minimal pairs, contractions, weak forms)

Use them to represent people:

- colleagues, friends, relations, members of a board or negotiating team, executive personnel, office staff

Use them to represent organisations:

- companies, departments, management positions, job responsibilities, liaison networks

Use them to represent places:

- layout of factory site, offices, shops, rooms in a house, village or city centre, airport

Use them to represent things:

- items of food and drink, cars, trains, planes, products, machines, parts, everyday objects, furniture

Use them to represent numbers:

- one, two, three
- 1st, 2nd, 3rd

Use them to represent block charts

Use them to represent periods or points in time

Use them to demonstrate actions

- *pick up, pass, put down, take, give, hold, drop, leave, push, fly, drive, move, stop, empty, put back, fill, place, pick out, arrange, lay, stand* etc

Use them to demonstrate 'function' words

- *this, that, these, those, here, there, some, none, all, any, a few, many, if, when, before, after, but, although, however, therefore*

Use them to demonstrate comparison

- *long, longer, longest*
  young, younger, youngest

Use them to demonstrate prepositions

- *in, on, between, in front of, behind* etc

Use them to demonstrate action sequences

- *I'm going to . . . , I'm . . . ing, I've . . . ed*

Use them to practise functions:

- *Could you . . . ?, As you see . . . , I'd like . . . . How about . . . ?*

Auditing sound and spelling

Students often ask for unfamiliar words or phrases to be spelled out or written down. This is partly because they want the security of the written word, but also because of the mistaken belief that this will give them reliable clues to pronunciation. Particularly with elementary students there are problems of hearing: the student's search images, based on L1, or on the written word, do not match what they hear, and this creates uncertainty.

Laying out one 1 cm rod at a time whilst spelling the word provides the student with a tangible representation of the letters without at this stage committing them to writing. By pointing to the rods one by one the student can be prompted to recall the letters.

T	E	A	C	H	E	R

Auditing letters

Further techniques and options

This purpose could also be served by an alphabetic chart, but the advantage of the rods is that we can go on to use them to represent syllables and sounds. The same word or combination of words can be represented in syllables using the 2 or 3 cm rods. One of the principal dangers of spelling is the false impression it may convey of the number and length of the syllables in a word. Re-counting and discriminating the spoken syllables is therefore an excellent exercise for the student, for which the rods again provide a tangible focus without resort to phonetic script or mere repetition practice.

Auditing syllables

Syllables may of course be stressed, or contain diphthongs or long vowels. Stress can be indicated by placing a 1 cm rod on top of the appropriate 2 cm syllable, or by contrasting 1, 2, or 3 cm rods.

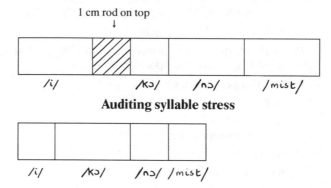

Auditing syllable stress

Vowels in a diphthong can be highlighted using 1 cm rods and practised first separately, and then together.

Auditing diphthongs

Contrasts between short and long vowels can be represented by a 'minimal pair' of rods. The student practices aural discrimination by listening to a word and pointing to the right rod. Oral discrimination can be practised by asking the student to alternate sounds or words (eg *ship* and *sheep*) at random. The teacher then points to the rod representing the sound actually made by the student (or not pointing at all if the sound falls in between or outside the range of the minimal pair).

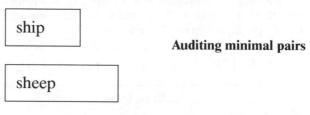

Auditing minimal pairs

A 1 cm rod representing an unvoiced consonant can be transformed by placing another 1 cm rod, signifying voicing, beneath it.

Auditing voicing

In this way we can also highlight vowel elongation before a voiced consonant.

The rods lend themselves well to the demonstration of contractions and liaison. The contrast between the word chain and the syllable chain can be shown by moving final-letter rods or by using two chains of rods, one for the words and another for the syllables.

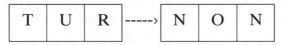

Auditing liaison

Students can be asked to 'audit' the stress pattern in a sentence using 1 and 2 cm rods ('Rod dictation').

its	time	we	went	to	di	nner
di	da	di	da	di	da	di

This applies also to intonation patterns, in which pitch is represented by displaying the rods on two or more levels.

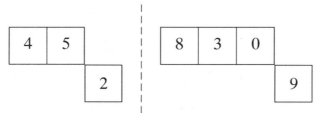

The above example also illustrates the division of an utterance in 'sense groups', in this case the two parts of a telephone number.

Summary

These are some of the most basic ways in which the rods provide the student with a tool for auditing the spoken word as well as, or in contrast to, the written.

The principle is that the student 'writes' with the rods, not just letters or words, but also sounds and syllables, stresses and liaisons. Since both teacher and student can write 'in rods', the student can also be asked to 'read off' the rods and the teacher can give 'rod dictation', in which the student must point to, select and arrange rods to represent an utterance.

The pronunciation points covered here are by no means exhaustive, but use of the rods itself suggests many further possibilities for phonological work.

The rod board

The rod board is an ordinary flat cheeseboard (approx 30×20 cm) with wooden runners pinned across its surface. The parallel runners are spaced out so as to form grooves into which strings of rods can be slotted.

The board then provides an ideal aid for using the rods to represent words and sentences, lines of dialogue, individual expressions and structural or functional substitution patterns. A 20×30 board will for example allow six lines of dialogue to be represented neatly and in straight lines.

It can easily function as a substitute for the whiteboard in one-to-one work, positioned on the table between teacher and student with the box of rods next to it. Its primary value is then to serve as an aid both in listening (representing the words which the student 'catches' from a recording) and recall or practice of expressions (in which the student lays out and/or 'reads off' the words of an expression one by one). Gaps in the student's recall or comprehension of the words heard or being practised can be indicated on the boards by gaps between the rods. Superfluous or missing words can be literally pointed out by the teacher.

7. Dictation

- Use it as an alternative to providing the student with a photocopy or printed text.
- **Teacher as dictaphone.** Student gives instructions such as 'Stop', 'Rewind to beginning of sentence', 'Go back to . . .' and takes dictation at his or her own rate, without the teacher needing to slow down in speech.
- **Auto-dictation (1).** Excellent for revision or presentation rehearsal, or just for re-writing notes. Consists of four stages:
    1. Student reads a line or listens to a line on tape.
    2. Without looking at the text student repeats line mentally and thinks the meaning.
    3. Student writes down the line or word from memory.
    4. Finally the student can check his or her dictation from the original notes or text.
- **Auto-dictation (2).** Teacher reads line from text. Student repeats and records on tape. Student then transcribes text from his or her own-voice recording and compares with original.
- **Keyword dictation.** Teacher reads text aloud. Student writes the most important content words, and reconstructs or summarises text from these.
- **Intensive dictation.** Student writes down every instance of a given language feature. For example all the past tense verbs, all words containing a particular phoneme, all phrasal verbs, all verb phrases used to refer to the future, all adjective-noun collocations etc.
- **Gapped dictation.** Teacher reads aloud leaving out all instances of a given language feature, for example all prepositions or past participles. Student fills in gaps in text from listening to tape or dictation by teacher.
- **Correction dictation.** Teacher includes factual mistakes in a dictation from known material for the student to correct.
- **Punctuation dictation.** Teacher reads without punctuation pausing.
- **Dictation sorting.** Teacher reads a list of words or phrases, for the student to sort into two or more groups. For example, sorting by tense, function, phonemics or intonation pattern.
- **Dictation matching.** Student pairs every word or phrase dictated with a list of matching words or phrases. For example matching comment and response, question and answer, sentence and tag, or matching by rhyme.
- **Picture, graph, or object dictation.** Student recreates the original from description by teacher, eg a Lego construction.
- **Cuisenaire dictation.** Student arranges rods (see page 121) according to the syllables, stresses and liaisons of the dictated utterance and then reproduces the utterance by 'reading' the rods.
- **Transformation dictation.** Any transformation drill can be turned into a dictation exercise in which the student transforms in writing.

Further techniques and options

- **Combined transformation-substitution dictation.** For example: teacher reads in 3rd person and student writes in 1st person.
- **Dictation to teacher, literal and creative.** Useful for typing up reformulated dialogues or student presentations in class. Can also be used as a method of reformulation in which the teacher feeds in new or alternative expressions as he or she types. Student then asked to compare original notes with copy produced by teacher and identify new language or alternative expressions.

8. Drills

To teach, through communication or to communicate through teaching? But do we really communicate through teaching?

Setting up a drill, or giving an instruction are forms of 'communication' except that very little is actually communicated. The essence of real communication is the dialogue, but how can dialogues be structured to carry a teaching point and given a format that elicits student input, without them ceasing to be real dialogues?

The advantage of teacher instructing student to do something as opposed to addressing a student in a way that demands a verbal response is that the student enacts the teacher's language. This is an aid to learning.

The drill uses the form of instruction rather than address to get the student to speak

Say
Repeat
Ask me

The problem is that the student is instructed to do nothing else but speak, so there is no communication. Yet with a little elaboration this can be changed. Take the instruction *Say*:

Say after me
　　　　what the time is
　　　　　　　day it is
　　　　　　　month it is
　　　　　　　year it is

But what about:

Say who you are
　　　　what you think about . . .
　　　　how you felt when . . .
　　　　what you can see from . . .
　　　　something your boss often says
　　　　two things you like about yourself

Then there is *Say it . . .* :

Say it loudly/softly
　　　　silently/mentally
　　　　in a whisper/with your lips
　　　　in one breath/with pauses
　　　　in red/green/blue

　　　　as you would say it to . . .
　　　　as if you were happy/thinking aloud/pushing a snowball
　　　　as . . . would say it
　　　　as you would say it if . . .
　　　　as . . . would say it if . . .

　　　　meaning/without meaning it
　　　　with an English accent
　　　　while rubbing your chin
　　　　looking amused
　　　　secretively

Further techniques and options

But there are many other types of instruction we can give that neither demand an immediate verbal response nor a physical action, yet which can serve as a prelude to other activities.

Think of a person who always
something you would like to do but . . .
a situation in which you felt
you needed to . . . in English
two things that you can see
have
do well
want to achieve by
two people you know who speak English
can advise you about . . .
you see often
a place you'll never forget
you'd like to be
you've always wanted to see
you go to often
you're going to visit in the future
you're travelling to next month
you hold meetings in

Remember a time when . . .
a situation in which . . .
a conversation you had in which . . .
a phone call you made in English
to someone important

Imagine that time
you are there
you are . . .
you are a . . .
you are _____ing . . .
you're in/by/about to . . .
ten differences between us
a comfortable position

Find something/red/square/heavy/useful/rough/expensive
a word or phrase which means . . .
a line in which someone makes a request
refuses an offer
three references to the future
as many prepositional verbs as you can

Name three people you'll be speaking to in English
a place I don't know
your favourite meal
a profession you might have had
two things you could give a presentation on
the person you admire most
three qualities you bring to your job
two things that you want to have
five people that are important to you

And so we could go on: **describe, explain, observe, point out, list, draw, etc.**

In addition we have instructions which are directly useful in setting up a role play or enacting a presentation:

Describe   your role
the situation
who you are addressing
who else is present
where you are now
what you can see
how you are sitting/standing
how you will be introduced
who is on your side
what the audience wants to hear
what your main point will be
what your message is
what notes you have prepared
what else you have with you
what aids you will be using
what tone you will adopt
what response you expect
what questions you expect
how much time you will have
what your aim is
what the best thing is that could happen
what the worst thing is that could happen
how you feel
what the pressures are

By changing from first to second person this format can also be used by the student to brief the teacher, who acts as substitute for a colleague or trainee:

You will be addressing . . .
Your aim will be to . . .

Finally we have enactment commands as such:

Introduce yourself to . . .
                me to
                X to

Sell me . . .

Convince me you're right for the job

Convince me that . . .

Complain to me about . . .

                    factory
Show me round your office
                    home

Explain to me your *proposals*
                    marketing strategy

Tell me how to get to . . .

Give a summary of . . .

Interview me for . . .

Ask me about . . .

Pretend you're making a phone call to . . .
                    to . . .

Further techniques and options

> *Write a letter to . . .*
> *Imagine that . . . and I'm . . .*

The advantage of the instructional format is that it gives the student clear instructions, and with this a sense of security and of the teacher's authority.

It can be used with the first day format for example, instead of presenting the student with interrogations or what may appear as a confusing mass of written language.

Advantages of three-step drills

One-to-one allows unlimited opportunities to drill individual students according to need. Drilling seems to be the very opposite of authentic communication, but this is a superficial perception. For one thing drills provide a secure and predictable framework for language practice and speechwork that students, particularly at elementary levels appreciate. The activity also helps them to feel that they are learning. Secondly drills represent a type of rhythmic interaction between teacher and student. In class teaching this may promote group solidarity and rapport. In one-to-one it can actually promote teacher-student solidarity and rapport. Thirdly, drills are a 'minimal' aid like rods and walkman. They can serve as minimal formats for communication as well as 'practice'.

There are drills, and drills however. Substitution drills based on teacher prompts are a form of elicitation and as such tend to put the student in a one-down position. Then again, the typical drill construction is a two-step one: prompt and utterance, question and answer, address and response. Even with transformation drills in which the student turns positives into negatives, or changes the tense, he or she is only required to practise *one* form at a time, quite in contrast to the demands of real-life communication.

In considering drills for use in one-to-one, the number three is what counts. Three-step drills have the following advantages over repetition or two-step drills:

- they give almost simultaneous practice in at least three forms, instead of one.
- the teacher makes a full and equal contribution to the rhythmic interaction (thus modelling is also continuous).
- the three-step drill is cyclical, and does not require stops for role reversal.
- the three-step drill easily combines substitution and transformation.
- the three-step drill can provide a minimal format for dialogues and communication.
- the three-step drill lends itself to more effective and realistic functional work as well as structure practice.
- the three-step drill is a waltz, not a march!

Three-step drills

A three-step drill requires a six-turn cycle to complete. In this case we have a transformation drill, going from positive to negative to interrogative. For example:

Teacher	Student
1. *We work.*	2. *We don't work.*
3. *Do we work?*	1. *We work.*
2. *We don't work.*	3. *Do we work?*

After six turns both partners have completed the three-step transformation. At this stage substitution could be introduced, repeating the six-turn cycle as follows:

She works.	*She doesn't work.*
Does she work?	*She works.*
She doesn't work.	*Does she work?*

It can then be recycled through a further transformation:

She worked.	*She didn't work.*
Did she work?	*She worked.*
She didn't work.	*Did she work?*

Finally, substitution and transformation cycles can be integrated into the basic cycle, in this case the basic positive–negative–question cycle:

She works.	*She doesn't work*	(transformation)
Has she worked?	*She has worked.*	(new trans.)
He didn't work.	*Did he work?*	(new trans. and substitution)

So within the basic three-step drill (substitution or transformation) we can introduce further transformations and/or substitutions *at* every step.

For some reason the use of drills is associated with speed and mechanical precision rather than thoughtfulness and creative precision. This probably has to do with their role in classroom teaching, the so-called 'quick drill', and in language labs. In one-to-one especially there is time to exploit the drill for its true potential, not as 'language practice' but as creative speechwork.

Speed should never be a consideration that takes priority. Instead the teacher can take the opportunity for a highly conscious speaking with deliberate variations of emphasis, intonation, pausing, and tone of voice: using the words of the drill to mean different things. Using speech to say something different each time. Let the student set the pace, however slow this is, allowing both teacher and student time to put care and a heightened awareness of sound and silence into the formation of speech. In this way the drill can become a highly satisfying communicative interaction.

The teacher should model an understanding that drills are based not on the principle of repetition, but the principle of non-repetition: of never saying exactly the same thing twice, even though the words may be the same. In the integrated three-step drill, involving both progressive substitution and progressive transformation the words themselves change, giving extra scope for putting different meanings and situational images into speech.

This is particularly important, if, as is possible in one-to-one you record the three or more steps as a drill on tape, with gaps for student repetition and self-recording. This provides a form of oral homework for the student, or yet another thing that the student can get on with alone in lesson time, experimenting and auditing his or her own speech without the self-consciousness that the presence of the teacher might bring, but rather with a self-awareness that brings learning and sensitivity.

A number of examples of three-step drills are given on page 132. Teachers will easily see that many of these can be generalised, and that other examples, specific for an individual one-to-one student can easily be devised.

Sample three-step drills

Dialogues

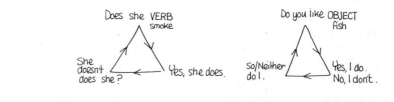

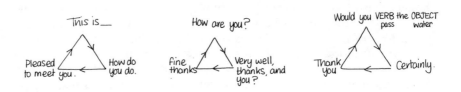

Lexis, Pronunciation and Grammar

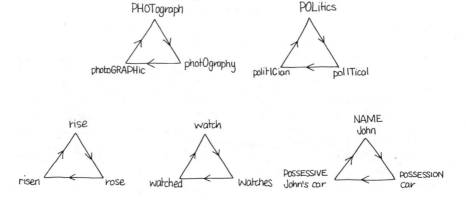

Build up

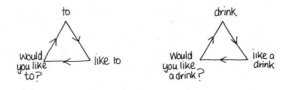

9. Reading aloud

Like drills and dictation, reading aloud is out of fashion as a teaching tool. More than this, it is regarded as a positively bad thing for teachers to encourage. This is particularly true as regards the teaching of English. English spelling being as it is, reading aloud is thought to promote sound/spelling confusion in the student, and reinforce bad pronunciation habits, as well as unnatural intonation.

Sooner or later however, students must face and overcome the problem of misleading spellings, and distinguish their image of a word as it is spelled, from their recollection of its sound. In reading aloud, the challenge is confronted head on and pitfalls abound. Precisely for this reason however we can *use* it to help students improve and master their typical pronunciation errors.

- Ask your student to read the text *syllable* by *syllable* instead of word by word, promoting awareness of liaison.
- Ask your student to read only the *vowel sounds*.
- Ask your student to read only words containing particular letters (eg '**o**' or '**u**').

For correction the teacher can use a phonemic chart, pointing with a pen to the appropriate sounds. The teacher can mark the student's problem words/sounds/letters on his or her own copy for review and more intensive practice.

Alternatively, or as a preparation for this procedure, the teacher can read aloud and ask the student to audit the syllables by marking liaisons, or audit the vowels by pointing to the chart.

Other options in reading aloud include the methods of 'auto-dictation' mentioned several times in this book, in which the student repeats a line silently and without looking at the text before speaking it.

You can ask the student:

- to utter each line in one breath.
- to step the text back into the past or forward into the future.
- to transform between 1st/2nd and 3rd person.
- to mime the text as if delivering it to an audience.
- to read not the words on the page but the images they evoke in the student's mind.
- to read a gapped text filling in missing words.
- to read it in different manners:
  as if to oneself
  mouthing only
  sarcastically
  as if bored/highly interested/shocked etc.

Slow readings by the teacher may be much appreciated by students who rarely get the opportunity to savour passively the individual sounds of the language.

These can be accompanied by relaxing background music or voiced artistically over louder or more dramatic music for psychological effect and penetration.

The teacher can vary the reading in countless ways, adding emphasis to pausing, to stressed syllables, to the vowels or to the consonants.

Further techniques and options

Manner and mood can be varied, as can register. The teacher can read an article, for example, as if reporting its contents to a friend in informal conversation.

Students themselves can be asked to read words or lines in the manner of their meaning, or to find physical gestures appropriate to them.

We should not think that reading aloud takes place only in the classroom or only when students are looking at texts. Many students give text-based presentations for example. And a large proportion of pronunciation faults arise because students are *mentally* reading aloud their own 'verbal images', without having been trained to read for sound, or to speak for *effect*.

10. Your language

Why do students learn so little from the teacher—from the teacher's own use of language rather than from what is formally 'taught' in the lesson? The weakness of a purely conversational approach to teaching and to one-to-one in particular lies in this phenomenon. Students are more concerned about their own performance than about listening to and learning from—auditing—the language that the teacher uses in addressing and interacting with them.

What does this talk consist of?

Questions

The teacher as interrogator, or even inquisitor. An easy trap to fall into. The danger with questions, however, is that even though students may understand and respond properly, the forms very rarely register in the student's mind except in cases where they are not understood. In other words the intruction *Now ask me* frequently gets a bewildered 'now-what-exactly-were-the-question-words' sort of look.

Speech Acts

The same applies to the teacher's natural or deliberate employment of functional language in speech acts ie when the teacher requests politely, suggests something, agrees with the student or even just greets him or her. Whatever language acquisition does take place it is not usually noticeable unless it is conscious: unless the student misunderstands or is for some reason surprised or intrigued by an expression the teacher used.

Classroom instructions and questions
Read, listen, repeat after me, write, look at . . ., What is this? Who are the speakers? Shall we go on?

Even with these, the student who understands is likely to focus on the content and not on the form of the question or instruction.

This is a pity in one-to-one where the student is exposed to so much teacher talk, either in the form of classroom language or conversation.

As with the mother tongue, students listen to the message and not to the medium. What seems to be lacking is the skill of conscious acquisition of language that is understood, transparent, but therefore also unheard!

Listening practice that focuses on understanding misses the point here. Auditing means conscious listening:

- to form as well as content
- to medium as well as message
- to sound as well as sense
- for novelty in language rather than in communication
  (*how* something is said rather than the intent with which it is said)

Physical instructions

As used in demonstrative teaching, and in the Total Physical Response method. Here the student is called upon to enact physical commands and action sequences. The difference that this type of instruction makes is that the focus is on the teacher's language and not on the student's own verbal response to that language. This puts the student in the position of

Further techniques and options

auditor, enacting language which is usually simple or carefully formatted for step by step elaboration.

Practical suggestions

1. Make a list of language you use or can use with a student. Adapt it to include as much language that you wish to teach as possible. Choose patterns for requests, offers, suggestions, advice, reassurances, instructions to introduce naturally language useful for the student. Some examples:

> *Let's . . .*
> *Shall we . . .*
>
> *How about . . . –ing*
> *Why don't we . . .*
>
> *Would you like to . . .*
>
> *It might be a good idea to . . .*
> *If I were you I'd . . .*
>
> *Could you. . .*
> *Could you try to . . .*
>
> *I'll just . . .*
> *I'm going to . . .*
>
> *Are you sure?*
> *Can you be more specific?*
> *Really?*
> *I see.*
> *I see your point.*
> *I'm not so sure.*
> *Do you really think so?*
> *What's your opinion?*
>
> *How are you today?*
> *How was the film/play/concert?*

2. Make a list of 'programming instructions' that you commonly employ in teaching. For example "Listen to the tape" "Look at the text" "Repeat" "Answer the questions" etc. See how many patterns from (1) you can use to bring useful language into your instructions. See how many instructions you can reformulate to bring in new verbs and other useful vocabulary or structures.

3. See how many new types of instruction you can think of that may be useful for the student in the learning process. For example:

> *Mentally repeat*
> *Listen only to the sounds*
> *Visualise the situation as you see it*
> *Identify with one of the characters as you listen*
> *Ask yourself . . .*
> *Say it in one breath*
> *Imagine this scene . . .*
> *Find two things that are . . .*

11. Words, gestures and actions

Although the word 'words' may be a linguistically imprecise term I have used it here for two reasons. Firstly to avoid the implications of what is usually called 'pronunciation' ie mechanical training to produce a formal correctness of articulation. Secondly because most of the techniques listed here apply to everything that can be presented to the student as an item of language: from the shortest phoneme to a complex sentence as well as to items of lexis. In broad terms, there are countless ways in which a word, phrase or sentence may be uttered; countless things that can be done with it through speech, mind, and body. It can be said in different ways, thought in different ways and embodied with different moods or gestures. What follows is intended to inspire the teacher with ideas for adding depth and colour to the presentation of 'words' as sounds, as thoughts, and as deeds, and in this way to make full use of the natural tendency for student-teacher mimicry that exists in one-to-one. At the same time, of course, the techniques can be seen as an aid to memory, physical as well as mental, emotional as well as intellectual, imaginative as well as rational.

Say it in different ways:

1. Sitting down or standing up.
2. Loudly, softly, quickly, slowly.
3. Mentally, silently with the lips, in whispers, with the voice.
4. Using forward and backward buildup of syllables.
5. Say it as an affirmation, a negation, a question.
6. With different 'mood gestures': neutrally, excitedly, sympathetically, reassuringly, mysteriously, tentatively etc.
7. With different 'vowel gestures': in a key of intoned 'AAAAAH!' (wonderment or vulnerability), or 'OOOOOH!' (incredulity or fascination). 'EEEEEEH' (fear or anxiety).
8. Stretching the vowels or stressing chosen consonants for effect.
9. With pauses before the main stress: *'Infor . . . MAtion'*
10. With falling or rising intonation.
11. Stepping the PHONEMES across the room.
12. Stepping the FEET, placing the right foot down on major stresses. ('Taking it in one's stride').
13. Rising and descending on the instep to add intonation patterns.
14. Holding speech in (as if talking to oneself) or sending it out on the breath.
15. Saying it in a single outbreath or mentally repeating with the breath held. The former is particularly useful for 'staccato' speakers.
16. Saying it as an act of releasing, throwing, offering, or focusing or shaping the word IN THE AIR ('voice projection').
17. Saying it with definite mental images: of the sounds
                                                of the spelling
                                                of the situation
                                                of the role or persona
18. Colouring the sounds or the breath (*Say it in red/green etc*)

Further techniques and options

19. Saying it to different people *(How would you say it to . . . ?)*

20. Singing it.
The general principle here is *'Say it in the manner of the meaning'.*
This can be applied to all sorts of words and language: nouns, adjectives, prepositions, verbs and adverbs, functions etc.

21. Say it while doing something else (picking something up, lighting a match, opening a book etc).

22. Extend the word in different ways:

by free association

by collocation

by rhyme

by word chains
(find a new word starting with the last sound or letter)

by addition of modifiers, prefixes, verbs, objects etc.

by identification ('If I were a tree I'd be an oak')

by embedding in stories, sayings, poems

by extending the category or set *(dog . . . cat, mouse, horse)*

23. Extend by listing derivations:

Pȯlitics, polĭtical, polĭtician, polĭticise, polĭtically
Econȯmics, econȯmic, ecȯnomist, econȯmically
Anȧlysis, analẏtical, ȧnalyst, ȧnalyse, analẏtically

24. Then ask the student to create combinations:

Political analyst
Political economy

In this way develop the student's facility to pronounce and use terms such as *productive employment,* distinguish pro**dŭce** and **prȯ**duce, **pȧr**sonal and personn**ȧl** etc.

25. Build up technical vocabulary in similar ways, for example:

	mould	design
plastic	moulding	operations
injection	moulded	parts

26. Using flash cards:

with mother tongue on flip side (particularly useful for idiomatic expressions)

with name of the function on one side and examples on flip side

with gaps *(I've been in London . . . 2 weeks)* and solution on flip side

with questions and response on flip side:
How do you do/How do you do

with picture on one side and word on flip side

with diagram on one side (eg for prepositions or using timelines)

with sentences containing errors (typical for *this* student) on one side and correction on flip side with ordinary letters on one side and phonetic transcription on the other

27. Finding examples of the word:

> in the room (find something round)
> in an illustration
> in a picture or wall chart
> on a graph or technical drawing

Gestures and actions

1. Devise a set of gestures for the vowel sounds.
   Check that diphthongs can be easily accommodated and that short vowels can lead gesturally into long ones. Or ask your student to invent his/her gestures.

2. Dramatise the gestures by associating them with exclamations or moods (eg AH! for wonder).

3. Use gestural sequences of vowels as a physical exercise routine, a sort of 'speech gymnastic' to use as a standing-up break at intervals in the lesson.

4. Use the gestures as markers for silent pronunciation correction, and use correction as an opportunity to practise the gestures singly or in minimal pairs.

5. Teach sound before sense for short utterances: extract the stressed and/or linked syllables from the expression you want to teach. Ask the student to mirror the vowel gestures for these syllables, then mime and speak the stressed syllables alone before practising, or revealing, the utterance as a whole, for example:

/e/	/i/	/o/
se	di	dwot
He said	he'd	what?

6. The procedure for teaching vowel gestures is as follows:
   1. Teacher gestures silently and student mirrors
   2. Teacher gestures aloud and student mirrors and echoes
   3. Teacher enunciates the sound and student gestures silently
   4. Teacher gestures silently and student enunciates the sound

7. The English vowels are best practised in sequences or pairs of short and/or long vowels, involving a steady gestural progression from 'arms up' to 'arms down', and contrast of short jerky movements of hands and forearm alone with longer continuous movements of the outstretched arm.

8. Students can be asked to 'mime-read' utterances before speaking them. Correction then occurs in advance of practice rather than after it.

Mime and action sequences

Like sound gestures, mime and action sequences offer the teacher a vivid technique for involving the student in a 'total physical response' to words, encouraging non-verbal, physical, and associative mechanisms of recall.

Further techniques and options

To begin with the teacher chooses a sequence of actions and/or states which can be physically demonstrated or mimed. An example of a demonstrative sequence would be the steps in operating a cassette recorder. An example of a mime sequence would be 'what you do when you wake up in the morning/get to the office'.

One basic procedure is as follows:

1.   Teacher demonstrates or mimes the sequence, announcing each step verbally before enacting it, for example:

> Press the eject button
> Remove the cassette
> Insert the new cassette
> Set counter to zero
> etc

2.   Teacher announces each step and student enacts it.

3.   Student announces the steps and teacher enacts them.

As with all techniques, action and mime sequences present a wide variety of options. Steps can be 'announced' in a number of ways:

—using the imperative *(Press the eject button)*

—using *going to*

—using sequencers *(first, secondly, after that, now . . .)*

In addition, steps can be reported retrospectively or anticipated prospectively as part of a tense sequence:

—*I'll just open the door*
—*I'm just opening the door*
—*I've just opened the door*

Using a fourth option in which the student both announces and enacts each step would require in this case that he or she appropriately *time* the prospective, parallel and retrospective utterances.

Tense contrasts can also be highlighted. For example simple past and present perfect.

I've opened the door (with door still open)
I opened the door (having closed it again)

But no less important than such 'tense drills' is the use of action and mime sequences in providing valuable vocabulary with both topical unity (eg the sequence of actions in starting a car) and grammatical unity (eg phrased 'action' verbs such as *pick up, put down, hang up, take off* etc).

Situations can be anticipated imaginatively using mime sequences:

> *I am entering the room*
> *I am deciding where to sit*
> *I am pouring myself some water*
> *I am sorting through my papers*

The student can then synchronously announce the teacher's silent steps . .

> **You** *are entering the room*

. . . or enact them following the teacher's prompts.

If necessary such situational mime can be used as a form of covert or overt confidence building, preparing the student for a real-life challenge, such as giving an important speech.

It is worth pointing out that not only physical actions but also *mental states* and *language functions* can be mimed.

Mental states: *I am interested/bored/undecided/thinking carefully*

Functions: *I am offering him some wine*

Functional gestures can be used in much the same way as sound gestures:

1. Teacher mimes the function silently and student mirrors (eg indicates gesturally to student that he or she should do something)
2. Teacher gestures aloud, using the appropriate function and student echoes (eg *Could you . . .*)
3. Teacher mimes the function silently and student verbalises or vice versa.
4. Teacher reports, formalises, or instructs student to fulfil a function, using the communicative verb.

    Report: *I asked him to . . .*
    Formalisation: *May I ask you to . . .*
    Instruction: *Ask him to . . .*

This reflects the fact that language functions are 'self-reflexive': the names we give to them ('offering', 'suggesting', 'advising', 'recommending' are themselves vital items of vocabulary actually used in fulfilling them in a formal register:

May I advise/recommend/suggest

as well as in reporting a speaker's words as deed:

He offered me a cigarette but I refused

In one-to-one, mime and action sequences give the individual student more active involvement and speaking practice than they would in a group. They provide a 'get up and do it' dimension to lessons that both livens things up and provides the security of a drill. They can also be employed in conjunction with Cuisenaire rods, using the latter as substitute realia, for example for table realia and the language of the dinner table. Above all they can serve to introduce essential basic vocabulary to the beginner in a way that reinforces learning through action and gesture.

The simplest action drills for teaching vocabulary make use of the commands *'Draw a . . .', 'Write . . .', 'Point to . . .'.* For example the teacher announces that he/she will *draw* a square, then draws it and rubs it out. A series of shapes is drawn and rubbed out and the teacher then instructs the student to draw them in turn. Finally the student gives the teacher instructions. At this stage correction is automatic. If the shape drawn by the teacher does not correspond to the image in the students mind, he or she will automatically think again. This built-in stimulus to self-correction applies to all action sequences.

Further techniques and options

12. Graphs

The simplified graphs that follow in this section are intended as suggestions for teachers who may wish:

a. to teach the language necessary for the interpretation and presentation of statistical material

b. to use graphs as a simple means of illustrating the tenses.

The distinction between these objectives reflects a general contrast we can draw between Business English in a business context, and General English in a business context. Naturally, to teach the first we would want to use authentic material, either provided by the student or drawn from any number of easily available sources (for example the Economic Indicators section on the last page of The Economist).

There are a number of ways in which we can work with graphs as presentational or practice material for a wide variety of language points.

1. Dictation by student and/or teacher of a graph by verbal description only. (A number of examples of this sort of exercise can be found in *Business Contacts,* Pergamon.)

2. Miming verbs of increase and decrease: describing graphs in the air.

3. Checking or illustrating the tenses, especially the Perfect Tenses, and the prepositions of time that accompany their use, with board work.

4. Drawing graphs for verbal interpretation by the student and interpreting graphs that the student has drawn up to check understanding.

5. Using business software and exploiting the graphics facility.

6. Using the computer as 'blackboard' and programming presentation or practice material.

7. Using graphs in place of conventional 'time lines' to plot the time structures of ordinary language.

8. Using graphs to plot intonation patterns spoken by student or teacher.

9. Using graphs to plot habits (adverbs of frequency).

Here are some examples of possible graphs, with associated language and activities.

Basic vocabulary

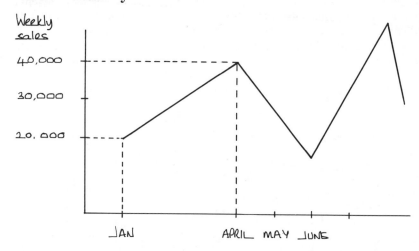

Notice the language:
- Nouns   (*increase, fall, decrease*)
- Prepositions   (*in* sales, *of* 20,000 units, *between* January and April)
- Modifiers   (*dramatic, marked, slight*)
- Adjectives   (*rapid, sudden*)
- Idioms   (*high point, slump, to rocket, to level off, to bottom out*)
- Adverbs   (*greatly, marginally*)

Verb forms

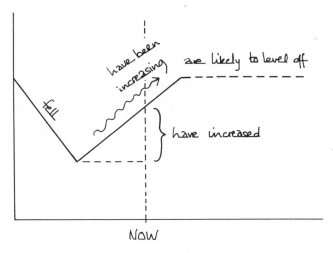

This graph illustrates verb forms, while the next uses personal details for the graph, allowing the language to be personalised.

Personal characteristics

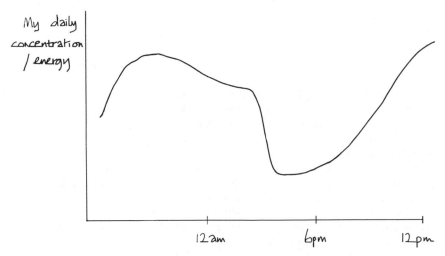

Here the alternative format is of course tabulation or block graphics. All forms offer opportunities for the personalisation of language and also intensive listening exercises. You will find many examples in *Business Contacts.*

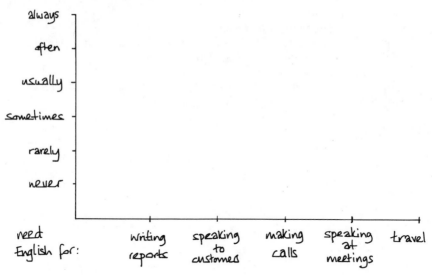

More imaginative use of graphs can be made by plotting personal or product characteristics:

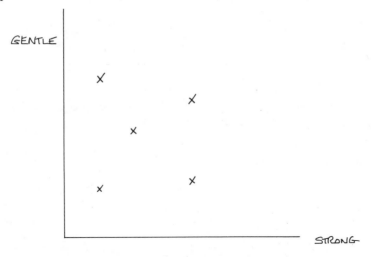

The marked points represent different individuals. These could be colleagues or friends, politicians, or even products (washing powder). The graph provides opportunities for practice of comparatives and superlative, conjunctions and contrast terms. (". . . as strong as, but not as gentle as . . .") ("gentler than, but not as strong as . . .").

You may want to think of other uses of graphs and tables. Providing the student with an exercise book containing graph paper and lined paper on opposite pages is an excellent way of improving note-taking. The graphs serve as prompts for the student's own revision work, with the written examples as the 'key'. Together they constitute a businesslike record of points covered in the course.

13. The student's mother tongue (L1)

Individual students have a particular L1, and advantage should be taken of this. You will be surprised how much more you can discover by yourself from one-to-one teaching than is found in reference books. One-to-one also offers greater potential for using knowledge both of typical L1 mistakes, and, more personally, of particular mistakes which the individual student makes.

Individual teachers, or schools, should build up a file, or system of files, of common errors shown by different language groups. These files should be organised according to particular types of error so that material is available quickly for individual students who exhibit particular problems.

A suitable system for such a file is suggested below.

1. Sounds unfamiliar to speakers of a given language.

    /s/ — /ʃ/ for Spanish speakers

2. Problem letters of the English alphabet.

    i and **e** for most students

3. Letter/sound confusions.

    very well **v/w**

4. Pronunciation faults and their correctives.

    Spanish /d/: model the tongue with your hands.

5. Reference words in the students L1 for the pronunciation of English sounds.

    ingenieur

6. 'False friends'; not just vocabulary but structures which are easily mis-heard and mis-spoken.

    aktuel

7. Basic differences in speech formation between L1 and L2.

    nasalisation; vowel elongation

In addition to an error file, other resources for a particular L1 could also be helpful:

1. Pronunciation sorting exercises. Student sorts words according to pronunciation, either in writing or from dictation. Testing or checking by dictation to teacher.

2. 'Spot the error' exercises, based on the typical mistakes of a particular student. Here is an example worksheet for a German student. Correct and incorrect sentences can be mixed. Typical mistakes in functional language as well as structural mistakes can be included. By including several examples of a particularly common or idiosyncratic error unnoticed by the student attention can be focused on this. Ask the student to identify a group of similar mistakes on the list.

Sample remedial worksheet for a German student

Correct the mistakes:

You mustn't eat everything!

I saw him before two weeks.

Further techniques and options

He has worked for us since three years.

In the last time inflation has gone down.

We met us at the airport.

What do you mean about it?

He wants that you ring him.

The both answers are correct.

The figures are the same like last year.

I would buy a pullover.

Correct tense?

I'm going to work by bus every day.

Her English improved this week.

'When' or 'If'?

... we don't receive a reply we will have to take further action.

... I go back to Germany I will feed my plants.

... you find it boring don't do it.

... you don't stop overworking you'll have no energy left for living.

... you don't know a word, look it up in the dictionary.

Show him in ... he arrives.

Please inform us ... you can't make it in time.

Give my regards to Peter ... you see him.

3. A beginner's knowledge of your student's language is enough to set you on the road in preparing bilingual materials or using bilingual formats as part of your teaching. Phrase books and dictionaries as well as books for beginners can all serve you.

4. Ask your student to prepare a two page list of language he or she feels important to know in L2. You can work on translating the items together, or refer to another teacher or to specialised reference sources if necessary.

5. Books or software for teaching English beginners a foreign language can be studied and utilised by reversal, for teaching beginners at English. This may be welcomed by a particular student or it may be inappropriate. As in all other matters, the use of bilingual approaches should be decided on an individual basis and not by theoretical prejudice.

6. Exploit biligual editions of poetry and short stories and bilingual company material.

7. Allocate teachers to students according to familiarity with the student's mother tongue, wherever possible.

8. Make sure students have dictionaries, bilingual as well as mono-lingual.

9. Make sure your school does too, in sufficient supply. One French dictionary for three one-to-one students is not enough.

10. Know where to obtain specialised technical dictionaries in libraries and bookshops.

11. Translation texts for work on by or with the student. This can be

extremely useful to highlight points via comparative/contrastive grammar. You may also have students who are preparing for exams requiring translation work, or who regularly are called upon to do translation as part of their job (secretaries are especially vulnerable to this problem).

How effectively you can do this work will depend on what sort of material is to be translated and on your familiarity with the student's L1. For biligual teachers it is an opportunity not to be missed, particularly valuable for idiomatic or specialised language that the student first provides in L1.

"Grammar-translation"

The one-to-one student is a monolingual 'class' of one. This means that the teaching lends itself to the use of bilingual teaching methods.

Not all students, particularly mature or older beginners are comfortable with direct or communicative teaching methods. A lifetime's use of L1 means that for them, language is associated with *their* language, *meaning* with L1.

Bilingual techniques are not just a way of providing security for this type of student. They also allow us to release and transfer the immense charge and reservoir of meaning embedded in the mother tongue to the target language. Teaching can be geared to *specific* contrasts between the grammar and lexis of the two languages, and this is where knowledge of the student's mother tongue has decisive advantages.

Recent researches suggest that beginners often need a so-called 'silent period' of passive assimilation of language before they begin to produce it. Direct and communicative teaching on the other hand, creates a lot of pressure on the student to produce language for 'practice' purposes right at the beginning. This pressure is magnified in one-to-one even though it may be not at all productive *for* the student.

The use of bilingual formats for the presentation of material and an element of grammar-translation reduces this pressure and provides a *cognitive* base for future language production. Unfortunately the term 'grammar-translation' is associated with a dry, mechanical and authoritarian approach to teaching. It is thought of as learning by fiat and explanation whereas in fact it can be one of the most interesting ways of learning by discovery and communication. Far from being merely a textbook-based method of instruction it can make use of a whole variety of authentic material:

—bilingual company brochures
—newspapers
—business cards
—children's books
—menus
—short stories and poems in bilingual editions
—transcripts of Reformulation from L1
     (ie the student as source of material)

To take the simplest example possible of a bilingual lesson we can think of the following: A Spanish student is asked to identify and mark the cognates appearing in his own bilingual company brochure. From this he discovers a list of Spanish words ending in *-cion* which are all cognate with English words ending in *-tion*. By listening to the teacher pronounce the English cognates he can also discover for himself a rule of thumb regarding the positioning of the stress, which in English tends to be on the penultimate syllable rather than the final one.

The student in other words, can be led to discover transformation rules of all sorts for him- or herself. The starting point is a bilingual or 'parallel' text, from which a set of cognate words or phrases is extracted by discovery. From this 'parallel' list one or more transformation rules can in turn be extracted and re-presented in the form of a diagram or chart. The parallel list, together with the transformation rules can then be used as a cognitive base for monolingual exercises or communication practice, and/or, as the raw material for a reconstruction of the L2 text ('reconstruction-translation'). Brainstorming can also elicit more examples (eg of words ending in *'cion'*) to which to apply the transformation rule.

Grammar-translation by discovery:

1. Parallel text
2. Extraction of parallel list
3. Representation of transformation rule
4. Extension of list and practice of rules
5. Reconstruction-translation of part or whole text, or extension of rule to further sentences in the text.

Alternatively the starting point may not be a text but a list, and/or a transformation rule represented in the form of a useful chart. From these teacher and student can work together on the translation of texts from L2 *or* L1 or the parallel composition of texts in L1 *and* L2, so that the *result* is a parallel text.

Parallel texts, L1 and L2

- Teacher reads L2 version for gist comprehension.
- Teacher reads L2 version and student writes down all words he or she can identify.
- As above with teacher as tape recorder (student can give instructions like *Stop/Go back to/Repeat the last sentence* etc.).
- Teacher gives slow reading with student following text (both L2).
- Teacher gives slow reading in *L1* with student following L2 text.
- Teacher gives 'concert reading' voicing the L1 text over music while student follows the parallel text.
- Student completes a partial list of matching L1 and L2 words or phrases from study of the parallel text.
- Student and teacher create this 'parallel list' together (eg teacher divides board into two columns and puts an initial example up to prompt student).
- Parallel list created from only those words which are either new or useful according to the student.

Parallel lists (L1 and L2)

- Sorting by linguistic classification (eg nouns/verbs/participles/ adverbials).

- Extraction and analysis of repeating correspondences and contrasts between L1 and L2 (eg *voy a* for *going to*).
- Teacher reads L2 list aloud and student repeats.
- Teacher names items by number on list and student pronounces the word or phrase (this can be done for those items which the student failed to pronounce properly in the initial repetition drill).
- Teacher picks an item from L2 list and student recalls L1 equivalent from random.
- Student picks an item from L1 list and teacher must recall L2 equivalent.
- Teacher picks item from L1 list and student recalls in L2.
- If a bilingual picture dictionary with word lists is being used teacher can prompt by pointing to the item in the picture.
- Reconstruction-translation of L1 text using the parallel list.
- Structure practice built around the vocabulary in the list or practising structures it already contains.
- Story or dialogue composition from the list.
- Spelling or structure practice using rods.
- Dictation as either revision or as a way of introducing the L2 text or both.
- Cloze dictation.
- Dictation in L2 with some words or expressions left in L1 for student to translate.
- Reading aloud of L2 text by student with pronunciation correction by teacher (using chart, gestures or prompting with only a single vowel/consonant/syllable/stress beat or using rods).
- Dramatised reading/recording by teacher/student.
- Auto-dictation from own recording by student.
- Alphabetic listing and recall.

Sources of parallel texts:

1. Penguin parallel texts; selection of short stories (Spanish, Soviet, French, German and Italian).
2. Penguin bilingual poetry editions.
3. Company brochures in bilingual or parallel editions.

Direct sources of parallel lists:

1. Phrase books. The Sunshine Phrase books in particular (published by Paperfronts) are to be recommended for their functional classification of material.
2. Grammar handbooks on the student's L1.
3. The Hutchinson range of 'Gimmick' books:

> El Gimmick: Spanish as the Spanish speak it
> Der Gimmick: Gesprochenes Deutsch
> both by Adrienne Penner

4. The Oxford English Picture Dictionary available in bilingual editions.

14. Student visits—a check list

If students are in Britain on a language course, it may be possible to arrange visits which will be directly relevant.

- Check whether the student's company has subsidiaries, clients or contacts that it may be possible for him or her to visit. Even if not, it may be possible to arrange a meeting with a 'counterpart' ie a professional or company in the same field as your student. Your own personal contacts could be helpful here. Alternatively there is also the Yellow Pages and business directories. One word of caution however. A visit to a company which may be competing in the same market as your student might be met with suspicion or refused outright. Assurances may need to be given that this is not a spying mission!

- Leave as much as possible of the telephoning and/or writing for the student to do. How much will vary from case to case but a confirmatory telephone call by the student should be possible in all cases.

- Use any letters exchanged with the other party as authentic lesson material, and record any telephone calls that you make to them for lesson use also.

- Even if suitable dates cannot be arranged obtain any material that you can from the other party, such as brochures or trade journals.

- Prepare and rehearse your student for any telephone calls and for the visit itself. This will include necessary social language as well as questions that he or she may wish to ask, or may be asked. Reformulation methods will serve this purpose well.

- Students usually appreciate being accompanied on such visits by their teacher. If you are going along check in advance whether it will be acceptable for you to record the conversations which take place. This can provide invaluable material and save you from furious notetaking.

- Dress appropriately for the visit and advise your student on this also.

- Use the preparation for the visit as an opportunity to explore contrasts in behaviour, conversational and professional style that your student might need to be aware of if he is visiting in a foreign country. This is not just icing on the cake, but can actually save considerable embarrassment.

- Your role in the visit will probably be to smooth interaction. Otherwise stay in the background and let the student do the talking. Learn what you can from it that will be useful for you in the future.

- Apart from making use of any notes or recorded conversations you can also get your student to write a report on the visit and/or a letter of thanks.

- If the visit was a purely social one, or handled by the student alone, get his or her feedback on any language difficulties, or successes.

15. Checklists when preparing lessons

It is all too easy to fall into a pattern when preparing lessons for a particular student. Although there are many different things that can be done, or many different ways of doing the same thing, most teachers develop a particular style, and have certain favourite (and unfavourite!) activities. Earlier in this book I have discussed certain possibilities for one-to-one teaching in some detail. Here, as an aide memoire for the teacher, are simple lists of possibilities:

1. Student needs

Situational preparation	Discourse awareness
Topical language	Register
Confidence	Structural competence
Remedial work	Motivation
Speed of response	Listening skill
Exposure to authentic language	Social language
Pronunciation	Presentation skills
Learner training	Fluency practice
Working on errors	Functions of English
Responsiveness	Relaxation

2. Format for student input

Rods	Company/authentic material
Open dialogues	Partial scripts
Graphs and charts	Translation work
CLL	Letter writing
Telephone calls	Typed format
Reformulation	Student presentation
Coursebook material for parallel writing	Role play

3. Lead-ins and appropriate styles of lessons

In-tray	Conversational
Student teaches	Role play
Low key	Interview
Discussion	Dramatic
Solo work	Presentation
Problem solving	Analytical
Humour	High energy
Task orientated	Consultative
Informal	Listening
Seating	

4. Ways to encourage student language awareness

Early in this book I introduced the concept of auditing—helping the student to become more aware of language, and particularly the language which he or she uses. This awareness covers both strictly linguistic features and the relationship between the different skills. Too often language teachers think only in terms of the traditional four skills, listening, speaking, reading and writing. Here is a checklist to remind you of some of the possible auditing techniques:

Dictation	Student board work
Transcription	Active listening
Self checking	Scanning
Identification	Sorting
Coursebook activities and exercises	Self recording
Drills	Games

5. Products of the lesson

Too often teachers have only the general idea that the lesson has "succeeded" if the student is "better" at the end than at the beginning. But there are many products of a lesson—physical products, *specific* improvements in *specific* areas. Here is a checklist of likely or actual products:

Practice	New skills
Proficiency	Transcripts
Performance	Tapes
Competence	Cards
Reinforcement	Recall
Processing skills	Preparation for situations

A check-list of ideas discussed in this book

Equipment
> highlighters
> typewriter
> tape recorder and mike or walkman recorder
> index book or alphabetical dividers for collocations
> blank tapes
> music for background
> whiteboard and pens
> blank cards
> cuisenaire rods (and rod board)
> paper and 4-colour biros for student and teacher
> twin-cassette deck radio recorder

Basic Formats
> Formatted pages—diary
>> collocation dictionary (2 columns)
>> bubble pages for short dialogues
>> partial scripts with sentence heads or multiple-choice completion
>> function page; with headings such as *Suggesting*
>> brainstorming pages
>> needs-analysis charts
>> three-column pages for new and useful vocab
>> graph paper
>> sorting and matching pages
>> daily agenda pages
>> memo pages
>> pages for exercises with right-hand column for key
>> blank cards

> Space on tape for student presentations
>> recorded messages
>> open dialogues
>> drills
>> recording new vocab

> Rods to represent participants in a meeting
>> words
>> syllables
>> sounds
>> positions in an organisation
>> layout of a plant

Chair and room space for different seating arrangements
> get up and do it activities
> 'total physical response'
> action sequences
> role play
> using gestures for the vowels
> sticking copies of lesson materials and products on walls

Board space for student presentations

Further techniques and options

Basic Techniques
Preformulation using partial scripts, charts etc
Reformulation from L1/L2
        by teacher or student
        in writing or on tape
        retrospective or immediate
Reformatting   tables
        charts and graphs
        collocation dictionary
        cards
Recycling   story/dialogue/letter or memo/dialogue/role play/
        exercises/drills/change of person or register
Reconstruction from key words
        language points
        content and/or function words
        sentence heads
Recall and Reinforcement brainstorming yesterday's new language
        slow readings on tape
        readings voiced over music for
          'pseudo-passive' listening
        card games, card sets and card
          conversations

Basic Modes   Conversational
Receptive
Instructional
Consultative
Task setting
Negotiatory
Game playing
Physical (mime and action sequences)
Mysterious
Humorous
Didactic
Open-ended
Structured
Spontaneous and spot-teaching
Solo work by student

Auditing and awareness building
    dictation
    transcription
    sorting and matching
    identification
    aural cloze
    comparison of transcript and recording

Take-away Products
    Personalised texts and tapes
    Card sets
    Student dictionary and formatted language notes and
      exercises

16. Timetabling and course structure: the basic methodological issues

Probably one of the main conflicts felt by teachers working in one-to-one is between an eclectic approach, drawing on a variety of techniques and materials, improvised day by day, and a systematic approach, perhaps based on a course book or core course. This conflict forms part of a wider dichotomy in teachers' minds which can be schematised as follows:

Approach A	Approach B
pre-teaching	post-teaching
teacher input	student input
core course or course book	no core course or course book
materials based	technical based
use of published materials	use of improvised materials
structured daily timetable	no structured daily timetable
learning	acquisition
correction	little correction
focus on language form	focus on language content
communication through authentic teaching	teaching through authentic communication

The two most basic options in teaching methodology are to pre-teach or to post-teach. Pre-teaching presents language forms first. It is up to the student to fill these with content, or to the teacher to 'personalise' the teaching. Post-teaching provides 'formats' ie frameworks for student input, and communicative *use* of language, before this language is analysed, or even provided. The content comes first, and from the student. The teacher provides language, and the means to identify, analyse and manipulate this language. Instead of the sequence: teacher presentation, controlled practice, free practice, personal use, we have another, which starts with personal use and may end with material that re-presents or practises 'language points' or 'patterns'.

In the end however, pre- and post-teaching form a cycle in which what is post-taught on the basis of student input and teacher reformulation prepares or pre-teaches the student to reformulate accurately and fluently his or her own meanings in L2.

Pre- and post-teaching unite in a task-teaching, which, in one-to-one can be based directly on the student's real-life communicative tasks. We ask the student to **do** whatever he or she needs to do in real life, and provide space for him or her to **do** it. Our aim in doing so is not to test what the student has learnt but to discover the language he needs and provide it. Our aim is not to 'teach' language and then withhold it in order to exercise and test the student, but to simply **give** the student the language he needs, and then train him or her to make use of it without any withholding.

We give language in order to **train** skills instead of withholding language in order to **test** skills.

Teachers have no monopoly on language, and it seems absurd for it to be 'taught' to students in measured doses. Teachers do have specialist skills in identifying language patterns and learning needs and it is these they are paid to share. For it is *the same skills* that the teachers apply in preparing lessons that the student can use in learning language. These are skills of identification, of language 'auditing'.

That is why I prefer to speak of reformulation and auditing rather than 'correction' and 'monitoring'. 'Correction' implies a certain one-upmanship on the part of the teacher. 'Monitoring' that the student must internalise this teacher correction.

Reformulation, on the other hand, tests the teacher's capacity to meet the student's requirements and not vice versa. Correction is haphazard; reformulation structured. Similarly 'monitoring' implies negative self-correction; 'auditing', however, is the student's positive discovery of language points and patterns.

Earlier in this book I gave one model of a teaching week based on the use of Reformulation. But the terms 'Reformulation', 'Preformulation' and 'Auditing' also offer a new picture of the use of published materials and core courses within a timetabled structure.

Example of a daily timetable

Lesson 1

Activity:	'Total Audit' of a structural dialogue (eg a unit from a *Streamline* cassette)
Materials:	Cassette only
Aids:	Rods and rod board
Technical Options:	—listening for gist
	—transfer of words to rod board
	—listening for key content words
	—reconstruction of function words by identification of grammar
	—transcription of complete dialogue by student
	—checking from teacher dictation
	—reinforcement by 'listening identification' with scene and characters
	—revision by reconstruction from content words only
	—practice of grammar with three step drills
	—role play by 'auto-prompt' (read, look up, speak)
Motive:	To start the day with 'receptive' work requiring attention but no excessive output from student. To use material with colour and humour. To exploit the natural interest of the student in 'What am I going to hear?' and his/her desire to understand English conversation
Mode:	Relaxed but alert, with teacher in spontaneous mode (giving help when required and drawing out the student's guesses, developing language points as they arise etc)
Result:	By the end of the lesson the student can hear, understand, and transcribe without help the words of a dialogue which was initially incomprehensible. In the

process he or she has worked on important structure, increased vocabulary, and has an enhanced awareness of the activity and micro-skills that go into listening (anticipation, mental reconstruction, identification of key words, imagination etc)

Lesson 2

Activity: Use of a Pre-formulated functional dialogue from a core syllabus

Materials: One blank cassette

Aids: rods and rod board

Technical Options: —dictation or elicitation of skeletal format for dialogue

—dictation or brainstorming of functional expressions

—sorting of a list of expressions into functional categories

—improvisation of dialogue from functional skeleton

—reformulation and recording (using rod board to practice lines before student records)

—use of taped dialogue as an open dialogue (student stops tape and anticipates response lines)

—transcription from the recording

—adding to the recording (eg repetition drills of functional expressions)

—three-step drills as appropriate for functional exchanges

—situational prompts for language transfer (student reads a 3rd person description of a situation in the 1st person and role plays what he/she will say)

—reading dialogue aloud in reported speech

Motive: To practice functions of social/business English without an intimidating coursebook. To raise awareness of language functions as reported speech. To create a tape with the student that he/she can use for self-study and practice

Mode: Structured work that creates its own materials and physical end-product

Result: Student goes away with the end-product tape and with the feeling of having mastered another 'unit' of a course without dependency on, or mechanical processing through, a coursebook.

Lesson 3

Activity: Student talk or presentation

Materials: Blank cassette

Aids: rods and rod board

Further techniques and options

Technical Options:

1. Preparation (see 'Topics for Talks' and 'Presentations')

2. Reformulation

	Teacher	Student
a		Speaks
b	Listens, makes notes and stops student at intervals to reformulate what he or she has said	
c		Records reformulated sentence

3. Use of cuisenaire rods
   To help the student remember the reformulated sentence the teacher can lay it out as a string of rods. Here the rod board is a valuable aid.
   The student practices the reformulated sentence by 'reading' it aloud from the rods.

4. Transcription
   The student listens to and transcribes the complete presentation from his or her own recording. Here again the rods come in useful. If the student is unsure of what he or she hears, the rods can be used to represent whatever words he or she thinks were said on the recording. Teacher can then prompt or correct by pointing to, adding or subtracting rods.

5. Dictation
   — Instead of recording the reformulated sentences teacher or student can write, or type them directly.
   — Teacher dictates the text of the reformulated presentation leaving out all the function words and dictating only a sequence of content words without punctuation.
   — Student then records a reconstruction of the presentation putting in all the missing function words (articles, prepositions, pronouns etc).

6. Reading aloud
   — Student reads a sentence or part of a sentence from the text of the reformulated presentation, repeats it silently without looking at the text and then either checks with the text first again or records the words from memory.

   As with the dictation exercise in (5) playback then makes the student aware of the sort of words he or she tends to ignore.

   This will be useful when the student prepares a set of cards or a sheet of prompts or keywords for delivering the presentation from. Usually when asked to prepare their own notes or prompts students focus only on content and content words, even though this is what they have *least* difficulty in remembering. It is the function words that count in their language learning and in effective delivery.

   This last lesson is a summary of one-to-one techniques as presented in this book. It could be followed by a lesson in which student and teacher engage in a 'Total Audit' of authentic reading matter: either an article or a transcript of a student talk/presentation. (See 'Auditing Texts'.)

In his book *Images and Options in the Language Classroom,* CUP 1986, Earl Stevick shows how "Options are more basic than Techniques".

My aim has also been to present the options that surround any given technique, activity or material.

Any activity is really a programmed sequence of options selected from various techniques. Dictation, for example, is a 'technique' which on closer examination reveals a multiplicity of different options each of which can form a useful part of a lesson procedure or activity. Preformulation, Reformulation, and Auditing represent 'master techniques' within which an even larger number of options circulate. The selection and use of these options is aimed at developing the micro-skills of the student in a way that clearly benefits the macro-skills of 'reading', 'writing', 'listening', and 'speaking'.

The sample course timetable I have presented could have been described quite differently:

Lesson 1
Streamline Connexions Unit 43
Objective: To practice the present perfect continuous

Lesson 2
Offering and suggesting

Lesson 3
Fluency practice: student talk

Lesson 4
Reading
The trouble with this sort of description, useful though it is as a shorthand, is that it *says nothing* about

— what the teacher is really doing

— how the teacher is doing it

— the methodological stance of the teacher

— its relation to one-to-one teaching

— the skills the student is practising

— the results and products, tangible and intangible

— the benefits and meaning experienced by the student

The language in which the lessons are thought and described prevents us, in other words, from saying what the lessons are really about, and from touching the real 'issues and options' of one-to-one.

In my view what the student is really learning to do is to 'audit', 'preformulate' and 'reformulate' language in communication. At the same time these words describe the very skills and 'master techniques' which the teacher applies to the job.

In this sense we are not so much teaching language as modelling the language skills which the student needs to communicate. Just as these skills break down into micro-skills so do our 'master techniques' break down into options.

It may be said that there is enough jargon in EFL as it is—why create more?

Further techniques and options

Jargon arises however whenever teachers *stop* looking for words to describe their experience of teaching and of the problems of individual learners, and instead rest content with a terminology that conceals issues and is remote from the actual experience of being with a student.

Writing this book has been a search for some words with which to *formulate* and also *reformulate* my approach to teaching one-to-one. In the process my teaching has changed for the better, and also transcended some of the dichotomies that the old language left me with.

But there is still a lot of psychological territory to be explored, as there is technical and technological territory. The use of hypnosis, for example, and the use of computers, . . . or both.

What is certain is that thoughtful formulation of the experience and possibilities of one-to-one is a potent source of reflection on the learning process as such.